D1490893

THE
SELF-SUFFICIENT
HOME

THE

SELF-SUFFICIENT
HOME

How to Provide for Your Family and Prepare for the Unexpected

NANCY HOFFMAN

Avon, Massachusetts

Published by
Adams Media, a division of F+W Media, Inc.
57 Littlefield Street, Avon, MA 02322. U.S.A.
www.adamsmedia.com

Contains material adapted and abridged from *The Modern-Day Pioneer* by Charlotte Denholtz, copyright © 2012 by F+W Media, Inc., ISBN 10: 1-4405-5179-0, ISBN 13: 978-1-4405-5179-6; *The Everything® Guide to Living Off the Grid*, by Terri Reid, copyright © 2011 by F+W Media, Inc., ISBN 10: 1-4405-1275-2, ISBN 13: 978-1-4405-1275-9; and *The Everything® Backyard Farming Book* by Neil Shelton, copyright © 2013 by F+W Media, Inc., ISBN 10: 1-4405-6601-1, ISBN 13: 978-1-4405-6601-1.

ISBN 10: 1-4405-8128-2
ISBN 13: 978-1-4405-8128-1
eISBN 10: 1-4405-8129-0
eISBN 13: 978-1-4405-8129-8

Printed in the United States of America.

10 9 8 7 6 5 4 3 2 1

This book is intended as general information only, and should not be used to diagnose or treat any health condition. In light of the complex, individual, and specific nature of health problems, this book is not intended to replace professional medical advice. The ideas, procedures, and suggestions in this book are intended to supplement, not replace, the advice of a trained medical professional. Consult your physician before adopting any of the suggestions in this book, as well as about any condition that may require diagnosis or medical attention. The author and publisher disclaim any liability arising directly or indirectly from the use of this book.

Many of the designations used by manufacturers and sellers to distinguish their product are claimed as trademarks. Where those designations appear in this book and F+W Media, Inc. was aware of a trademark claim, the designations have been printed with initial capital letters.

This publication is designed to provide accurate and authoritative information with regard to the subject matter covered. It is sold with the understanding that the publisher is not engaged in rendering legal, accounting, or other professional advice. If legal advice or other expert assistance is required, the services of a competent professional person should be sought.
—From a *Declaration of Principles* jointly adopted by a Committee of the American Bar Association and a Committee of Publishers and Associations

Cover design by Stephanie Hannus.
Cover images © Jenny Lipets/123RF; Jane Rix/123RF; Liliya Drifan/123RF.

This book is available at quantity discounts for bulk purchases.
For information, please call 1-800-289-0963.

CONTENTS

INTRODUCTION
Sustainable Living: Getting Back to Basics

Self-sufficiency means different things to different people. Some simply install solar paneling to reduce their electricity bills. Some find self-sufficiency in a backyard farm with a garden, small livestock, and grain storage that provide the fresh food their families need. And some may collect their own water, grow acres of crops, and tend livestock, all while utilizing natural and alternative energy sources to supplement—or replace—traditional gas, oil, and electric power.

Whether you want to tone down your carbon footprint or prepare for disaster, if you want to live a more responsible, eco-friendly life, without the harsh conditions and brutal work that often come with complete "off-the-grid" living, you'll find what you need to know in *The Self-Sufficient Home*. Throughout this book you'll find many practical tips that will teach you how to incorporate various homesteading methods into your current lifestyle, whether you wish to start with small projects, such as herb gardening and composting, or want to make a major lifestyle change, like buying a farm, planting multiple acres, and harvesting a lucrative crop. This practical and informative guide will ease you and your family into a more independent way of living—whether you live in the city, the suburbs, or a rural area—and give you enough of an overview to be able to make initial decisions and move forward in the right direction. Here you'll learn the skills you need to transition to a self-sufficient lifestyle, including growing and preserving your own food, managing debt, raising and tending livestock, and harnessing alternate energy sources. You'll even find a chapter on emergency preparedness, an essential resource during uncertain economic times, power failures, storms, natural disasters, or national emergencies. What you choose to incorporate into your self-sufficient lifestyle is up to you; ultimately, you know what is best for your family, your goals, and your needs.

So stop living a life filled with expenses, stress, and dependence on the grid. Instead, start living a life that lets you and your family stay safe, healthy, and happy and rediscover the simple pleasures of a self-sufficient lifestyle. Let's get started.

CHAPTER 1

Getting Started

So you're thinking about starting a self-sufficient lifestyle. You may want to supplement your current energy sources to lower your heating bills, produce more wholesome and healthy foods for your family, or simply reduce your carbon footprint. You may want to take larger steps too—starting your own backyard farm, raising livestock, or utilizing alternative energy sources to move your home off the grid. The options are numerous and we'll go over all of them throughout the course of the book, but where should you start? From dealing with debt to creating a sustainable budget to keeping your family safe, this chapter details the practical considerations you must recognize when creating a self-sufficient home.

LEARN WHY YOU SHOULD START A SELF-SUFFICIENT HOME

The answers are as varied as the individuals who choose this lifestyle. You may want to start a self-sufficient home because you're looking for a "greener" lifestyle and want to lessen your carbon footprint. You don't have to move out of town or even from your current residence to do this. You can install solar-energy shingles on your roof or a geothermal heating and cooling system in your home. You can consider designs for low-impact wind turbines that generate electricity. You can install energy-efficient appliances and low-water-use toilets and showerheads. Implementing many of these measures will not only make an ecological statement, but it will also save money in the long run.

Preserve Your Sustainable Lifestyle

Go green and ditch the bottled water. Bottled water has a huge carbon footprint; it's bottled at a central location in small plastic bottles and shipped all over. Try buying a reusable water bottle or canteen for your water. Many plastic water bottles are recycled, but most are not, making the footprint even bigger.

You may want to become self-sufficient because you are looking for a simpler, back-to-basics lifestyle. Perhaps the hustle and bustle of the city is too much. You want to raise your children at a slower pace in a place where they can grow up understanding the benefits of hard work and responsibility. You want to feel the pleasure of a pantry stocked with jars of your own homemade preserves and pickles. You want to walk outside in the early morning light and scatter feed to your chickens and collect farm-fresh eggs. You want to gather your own vegetables and grow your own meat. You enjoy the security you feel knowing your family would be able to get by, no matter what the machinations of the economy.

You may decide to start a self-sufficient home because you are concerned with security. You don't feel that the world is a safe place for you and your family, especially not in the large cities. You want to move to a place where you don't rely on power grids that can be destroyed in terrorist attacks. You don't want to be in a populated area where you might be a target for a biochemical or nuclear threat. You are becoming more independent for safety and to create a self-reliant lifestyle for yourself and the ones you love. You have a sense of urgency, and the sooner you can relocate, the better.

Finally, you might be considering a self-sufficient lifestyle as a necessary option because of a financial setback. Living a back-to-basics and no-frills lifestyle might be what you need as you look for new employment or work to get out from under an upside-down mortgage. Many of the things you will read in this book will help you save money and learn to economize. However, it is important to realize that starting a self-sufficient home is not an escape hatch for any financial issues: You are still responsible for resolving any owed monies or loans in your name.

Depending on your resources and your motivation, living self-sufficiently can be done quickly, or it can be done in a series of small steps. Either way, you need to be sure you have taken into account more than just solar power and dehydrated food. Moving from a life that is reliant on the ease and convenience of nearby malls and thermostat-regulated environments to one of making do or doing without, and chopping wood to heat your home, can be overwhelming. You need to be sure you prepare yourself physically, mentally, financially, and emotionally.

The good news is you can start today, no matter where you are or what you are doing. You can start looking at your finances to see where you can economize. You can look at your food preparation and substitute basic items for quickly prepared foods. You can take an inventory of how often you run to the grocery store, the coffee shop, or the fast-food restaurant and limit your exposure to any or all of them.

RECOGNIZE YOUR OPTIONS FOR SELF-SUFFICIENCY

What does "self-sufficient" mean to you personally? You can actually live this lifestyle in the middle of a suburb, if your version of self-sufficient is to be less dependent on traditional fuel sources. Installing a geothermal heating and cooling system along with solar panels and a battery array backup system might be your solution for an independent existence. You can also live independently by purchasing 200 acres of land in the mountains of Kentucky and creating your own self-sufficient environment. You can be completely self-sufficient by buying a small farmette and learning to raise some livestock and some vegetables.

The beauty of your self-sufficient home is that you get to determine what you want to do and how far you want to go. However, every successful adventure begins with a plan. List your goals and set down intermediate steps. Do you want to eventually move away from the city, but still need the employment found there? Perhaps your next step would be relocating to a smaller town near enough to commute to the city, with a larger piece of property to begin your first garden. Do you want to have a green home? Perhaps your next step would be to look into the geographic advantages of the different options of alternative energy.

Each goal you make and each step you take will bring you closer to your final destination in your own way.

CONSIDER PRACTICAL IDEAS TO KEEP YOU AND YOUR FAMILY SAFE

For many people, moving to a secluded spot nestled next to Yellowstone National Park with nothing but the pine trees, bears, and moose as neighbors could seem ideal. But, you need to realistically decide where your self-sufficient home will be located and what the extent of your independence will be. Here are some things you need to consider:

Health Care

If you are planning to have children, or already have children, you don't want to be 200 miles away from the nearest hospital, unless you have the kind of training or experience that makes you capable of giving emergency medical attention to your family members. And, even if you have that training, what happens if you are the one who gets hurt?

Cellular Phone Linkage

With modern technology and a good satellite provider, you can have Internet and television access almost anywhere in the world. The problem comes when you are trying to get cell phone linkage, because you need to be able to bounce off a tower. There are still many places throughout the United States and the world that don't have cell coverage.

Access to Mass Transportation

If you need to fly occasionally, you need to decide how close you want to be to an airport. Luckily, today there are a number of secondary airports that feed into major airports. Even a relatively small city like Dubuque, Iowa, has an airport that feeds into Chicago's O'Hare International Airport. Depending on how often you fly, you should decide how far you want to travel to get to an airport.

Access to "Civilization"

There are many other conveniences you might not want to sacrifice with your new off-grid lifestyle. Do you want to occasionally go to a movie or out to dinner? Will you need to go grocery shopping on a regular basis? Will your children take piano, ballet, gymnastics, or other lessons? Do you want to live near a library or in a college town? Remember, it's not realistic for you to believe that you could "commute in" for many of these activities. If you are living a completely off-grid lifestyle, you won't have time to spend several hours driving back and forth. You need to be brutally honest with yourself before you make any decisions!

SUSTAIN RELATIONSHIPS WHILE MAINTAINING INDEPENDENCE

Just because you are becoming self-sufficient does not mean you have to leave your friends and family behind. Especially today, with the technology available, it is easy to keep in touch on a daily basis.

Social Networking

Facebook, Twitter, and blogging are wonderful ways to share information, post photos, and keep up to date on the comings and goings of your friends and family. A quick browse through your Facebook page can update you on any changes or events in the lives of any of your "friends." Over the past year, the number of users in countries outside the United States, particularly in Europe, Africa, and Latin America, has grown significantly.

Video Chat and Video Conferencing

There are a number of software programs that allow you, with the use of a webcam, to hook up with friends and family all around the world for a video chat and even a video conference. Some of these programs allow for multiple chats at the same time, so you can connect with several friends all across the country and visit together via video chat. You will need high-speed Internet and a computer with webcam capabilities, but beyond that, the software is user-friendly and you can "see" your friends and family whenever you desire.

Make Room for Visitors

When you decide on your self-sufficient home, whether or not you move to a new property, make sure you've set aside space for visitors. A back-to-basics, out-in-the-country lifestyle appeals to many people, and even though they might not be able to choose this life for themselves, they are curious and eager to learn more. Most people who make the move find they often become a long-weekend destination for families and friends. Although the extra mouths to feed can be a little burdensome, these visits give you the opportunity to put your guests to work so they get a taste of what living self-sufficiently is really like.

DEAL WITH DEBT

Are there good reasons to go into debt? Certainly! If you are investing in something that will increase in value—a home, a business, or even student loans—that is good debt. If you take out a home equity loan to pay off a higher-interest credit card, that's a good debt because your home equity loan will generally have a lower interest rate and will be tax-deductible. However, be careful you don't spend your home's equity on bad debt such as a vacation, new furniture, or other items that will not increase or retain value. Most consumer debt, i.e., credit cards, is bad debt. A good rule to live by is: "if you can't afford to pay off your credit card at the end of the month, you can't afford to make a purchase."

Self-Sufficient Facts, Knowledge, and Support
It's important to know your credit score. Your credit score will dictate how much borrowing money will cost you. Each of the three main credit bureaus offers free reports each year. To get a free report, go to the website set up in accordance with the Fair and Accurate Credit Transactions Act (FACT Act) (*www.annual creditreport.com*).

CREATE AND STICK TO A BUDGET

The first step to getting out of debt is to see where you spend your money. If you find you have more bills than money at the end of the month but don't understand where it all went, a budget is an essential step. However, a budget will do you absolutely no good if you create it and file it away. You need to make daily entries into your budget until you have better control of your finances.

The first step in creating your budget is to pull together all of your financial information. This includes paycheck stubs, bank statements, bills, and any other expenses or income. Sort these into several piles: income, weekly expenses, monthly expenses, quarterly expenses, and annual expenses. The weekly expenses might be things like gasoline for your car, the cost of babysitting, or grocery shopping. A monthly expense might be a utility bill or credit card payment. A quarterly expense might be your garbage or water bill. And an annual expense might be your property taxes or vehicle registration.

First, create a list for income. In one column place the source of income; in the next column place the amount. If you are self-employed and your income varies, always use the most conservative amount. Don't forget to deduct self-employment taxes and any other fees you pay from your income. If you receive a regular paycheck, you should only count your net income, or the amount you receive after the taxes and other deductions are subtracted.

The next list will include your weekly expenses. This list will have three columns. In the first column, record the name of each expense; remember to include even the smallest items, such as the cost of your morning coffee or the amount you spend for lunch each day. In the second column, record your estimated costs for these expenses. Fill in the third column at the end of the week, when you tally your actual expenses and compare them to the second column.

Create lists for your monthly, quarterly, and annual expenses in the same way. Remember to include things such as car insurance, dry-cleaning costs, veterinary costs, entertainment, and anywhere else you spend money. Make sure to include every expense, no matter how small. Paying a few dollars a day for a coffee may not seem like a budget buster, but small costs like this add up to big numbers!

Look at your expenses and see which ones are fixed (the amount is always the same, such as a mortgage payment) and which ones are variable (the amount changes, such as a grocery bill). Highlight the expenses that are variable.

Now, add up the columns. If your expenses exceed your income, you need to look at your variable expenses and see which ones can be altered. You can also look at some of the luxury expenses, such as cable television, entertainment, or other nonessential charges, and decide which ones to eliminate. You need to put yourself in a situation where you are in control of your money, not the other way around.

Search for Alternative Solutions

If you have eliminated all nonessential bills and have cut your variable expenses as much as you can, and you still have more expenses than income, you need to make some serious decisions. Talk to your creditors to see if you can reduce your payments for the time being. Most creditors will want to work with you if they know you are trying.

Look at alternatives in some of your expenses. When was the last time you had your insurance policy updated? Could there be a savings in switching providers? Are you shopping at low-cost, no-frills grocery stores? Are you purchasing expensive convenience foods, or are you buying less-expensive ingredients to make meals from scratch? Are you buying items such as soft drinks, packaged bakery goods, and bottled water that you might be able to do without?

Maintain Daily Records

Finally, you need to keep a daily record of any money you spend. A small notebook or even an index card is fine for this purpose. Every time you make a purchase, from a candy bar or a pair of nylons to even giving the paperboy a tip, you need to write down the amount. At the end of the week, sort these amounts into the categories you've already created in your budget. Add the amounts to see if the estimate you placed in the first column when you created your budget is realistic or if you underestimated your spending habits. If you are like most people, you will be amazed at the amount of money that flows through your hands without conscious thought. If you are spending more than is budgeted, you need to curb your impulse spending, because that is the only way you are going to get out of debt.

Maintain your daily record-keeping for at least a month, so you have a good indication of where your money is going.

Stick to a Budget

Creating a budget is easy. Sticking to a budget is much more difficult. But, if you have a goal in mind, any sacrifices you make will be worth it. Use the following guidelines to make sure you create a reasonable budget to which you can adhere:

- First, be sure that both you and your partner agree to the new budget. Your budget will not work if one of you is not onboard. You need to support each other and work toward your goal together.
- Be creative. Find new ways to save money and get excited about it. Rather than going to the movies, rent a movie and pop your own popcorn. Try shopping at resale shops rather than at the mall. Make a list when you go to the store, and stick to the list!
- Be frugal. Look at the ways you might be wasting money. Do you leave the lights on in unoccupied rooms? Do you use energy-efficient lighting? Do you run hot water longer than necessary? Do you throw away leftovers every week when you clean out your refrigerator?

If your goal is to eventually become completely self-sufficient, you need to be not only frugal, but also resourceful. Think of ways you might be able to add to your income in order to get out of debt. Do you have a hobby or skill that could produce income? Are there part-time job opportunities that would work into your schedule? Are there items in your home that could be sold on Craigslist or eBay?

Make sure to revisit your budget often. The worst thing you can do is to create your budget and then forget about it. You need to be diligent and wise when it comes to your personal finances if you ever want to be independent.

SET REASONABLE FINANCIAL GOALS

As you pay off your debt, it is important for you and your partner to set short- and long-term goals. By setting goals, you will remind yourself of the ultimate reward for getting out of debt. Every time you save money or eliminate a creditor, you get closer to your goal.

Short-term goals are those you can accomplish within several months or less than a year. As you read through the rest of this book, think about realistic goals you can set that will move you closer to your ultimate goal of becoming self-sufficient. A short-term goal could be learning to cook using basic ingredients, or attending an alternative energy fair. Create goals you can accomplish as you work your way out of debt.

Long-term goals generally take a year or more to accomplish. A long-term goal could be purchasing a piece of property or installing an alternate energy source in your home. You can have several short-term goals leading up to your long-term goal. For example, researching the costs of solar panels and how to install them could be a short-term goal that complements your long-term goal of installing an alternate energy source.

Preserve Your Sustainable Lifestyle

Effective goals follow these basic rules: be positive in your goal statements, write down your goal and put it where you can see it every day, be specific when setting your goals so you can track your success, and set realistic goals.

Long-term goals should excite you and give you the incentive to work hard and sacrifice in order to realize them. Long-term goals can be as soon as a year or two away or can be as far as five years away. Setting a goal for more than five years can be a deterrent to your day-to-day efforts because the realization of the goal can seem so far away. If you believe you need more than five years to reach your goal, be sure to set some stepping-stone midterm goals to help you stay on task and motivated.

Either way, it is important that you create goals you can reasonably accomplish, but also set goals that are challenging. Nothing takes the wind out of your sails faster than failing to meet a goal. You don't want to get discouraged and abandon the whole effort. Paying off the remainder of your thirty-year mortgage in two years is unrealistic and an unfair burden to place on yourself and your family. However, placing a goal to pay off your $5,000 credit card debt in five years makes a mockery of your efforts. Although you shouldn't be creating goals that will discourage you, goals should make you stretch and challenge you. Aim for the most you can do.

TAKE BABY STEPS TOWARD YOUR SELF-SUFFICIENT LIFESTYLE

For many, just getting started seems overwhelming. You should start with baby steps such as the following to get you moving toward a more independent, self-sustaining lifestyle.

Reduce Your Energy Use

Look around and unplug all those unnecessary appliances. Use a hand-operated can opener instead of an electric one. Use a whisk instead of a mixer. Look for phantom electricity drains. The U.S. Department of Energy states, "Many appliances continue to draw a small amount of stand-by power when they are switched 'off.' These 'phantom loads' occur in most appliances that use electricity, such as VCRs, televisions, stereos, computers, and kitchen appliances. . . . These loads can be avoided by unplugging the appliance or using a power strip and using the switch on the power strip to cut all power to the appliance."

Self-Sufficient Facts, Knowledge, and Support
In the average home, more than 50 percent of the electricity used to power electronics is consumed while the devices are turned off! In the United States alone, phantom load costs consumers more than $3 billion a year and adds up to the output of several full-size power plants.

Check the Energy Star ratings on your appliances and, if you can, replace older appliances with more efficient new ones. If you can't afford to do that, inspect your current appliances. Be sure that seals are in good repair, or replace them. Make sure your washing machine belts are tight so the engine doesn't have to work harder to get your clothes clean and the spin cycles draw out a majority of the water. Be sure that filters in your furnace, air conditioner, refrigerator, and dryer are clean and allow free-flowing air. Also, check the air vents from your dryer to the outside to be sure they are clean and free of obstructions.

Plant a Garden

Whether you have a spot in your yard that can be tilled or some potting soil, a collection of containers, and a room on your patio or porch, you can plant a garden. Start with some tomato plants in a five-gallon pail or some herbs on a sunny kitchen window. Begin to learn the joy of growing your own food.

Many urban communities have been promoting "community gardens," or shared spaces in a public location, where residents can purchase a plot to use for gardening. This is a great solution if you live in a heavily populated city or simply don't have the yard space for a large garden. Just be sure to have the soil tested before buying, as lead and other toxic heavy metals are present in some community gardens.

Stop Eating Out

When you are busy and running late, it's easy to fall into the habit of driving through, picking up, and/or eating out. To learn to be more self-sufficient and to have a healthier life, plan a menu and learn to cook from the basics. Make your own homemade pizza or taco salad. Substitute healthier alternatives to high-fat, high-sodium fast-food offerings.

Control Your Food Sources

As a modern consumer, you don't have much control over the food you put in your family's mouths, but when living self-sufficiently, it's possible to have 100 percent control. If you are growing your own food and raising your own livestock, you don't need to worry about what pesticides are used on your food if you don't use any (which in all likelihood, you will not when you learn the natural and alternative pest-control methods found in Chapter 5), or whether you are consuming something you're allergic to if you know what ingredients are in everything you eat. Commercial meat animals are, by necessity, pumped full of antibiotics as preemptive protection against disease. In your backyard, however, you only need to concern yourself with the actual diseases, if any, contracted by a few individuals, so you don't have to medicate healthy animals unless they become sick. Not only are fresh, homegrown produce, meat, and eggs healthier and more nutritious than factory-farmed versions of the same products, but spending your afternoon in the garden is better for your mental and physical health than spending the same time in traffic or walking around a crowded mall or supermarket.

Start Studying

Now is the time to take a class at the local Cooperative Extension System office or community college or borrow books from your library about alternate energy sources, gardening, livestock, or any other area you need to brush up on. Sign up for seed catalogs and browse through the varieties available and the advantages and disadvantages of each.

Organizations also occasionally offer workshops and classes on making the transition to a more self-sufficient lifestyle. Sign up for some, and make it a point to talk to the teacher—more likely than not, he or she also lives this lifestyle and can give you some first-hand advice. Nothing beats the wisdom of experience!

CHAPTER 2

Alternate Energy Sources

A basic idea of self-sufficient living is to maintain a home that can sustain its own power, no matter what happens in the outside world. If you use alternate energy sources, whether solely or in tandem with traditional gas, electric, or oil sources, and the rest of the world loses power, you and your family will be fine. One example of the importance of having your own power source is the ice storm that hit Canada in January 1998. Over the course of six days, freezing rain covered Ontario, Quebec, and New Brunswick with 3" to 4" of ice. The ice coating caused electric wires to become brittle and break. The power outages lasted for as long as a month. More than 3 million people were without power in Quebec, and more than 1 million in eastern Ontario were as well. About 100,000 people went into shelters in school gymnasiums and churches. If you were living in a self-sustaining house with your own power source and heat source, you would not be one of those forced to relocate. As a matter of fact, if the grid went down, it would not affect your life at all. This chapter explains the various types of alternative energy available to you, including solar, biomass, geothermal, hydroelectric, wind, and even wood burning. Here you'll gather the information you need to choose, install, and maintain alternative energy sources that suit your needs and power your home.

LEARN ABOUT BIOMASS ALTERNATIVE ENERGY

Several centuries ago, many German farmers and their families lived in housebarns. These buildings were comprised of the barn on the ground level and the home on the second and sometimes third level. The primary reason for this arrangement was so that the warmth from the animals would rise up and help heat the home. That was one of the first uses of an alternative energy source called *biomass*.

Biomass is organic material made from plants and animals that can be processed in order to provide energy. It is processed by burning and by fermenting. The most common type of biomass that is burned is wood; however, garbage and wood waste (a wood byproduct) can also be burned to produce energy. Another common biomass product is methane gas.

Green Mountain Power (*www.cvps.com/cowpower*), a Vermont electricity utility, offers its customers the option to power their homes using Cow Power. Local dairy farmers gather cow manure into specially designed holding tanks called methane digesters that keep the manure at a certain temperature. The manure releases methane gas, which is piped into a generator that creates electricity.

Self-Sufficient Facts, Knowledge, and Support
One cow's waste can produce enough electricity to light two 110-watt light bulbs twenty-four hours a day.

Unless you decide to build one for yourself, methane digesters are only available for larger agricultural facilities. However, as more people explore the benefits of methane gas, small residential units may become available in the future.

LOOK INTO SOLAR POWER

There are two different kinds of solar energy: passive and active. Passive solar energy means you are not using any mechanical devices to harness the energy of the sun. For example, using south-facing windows to provide natural light would be passive solar energy. Having a sunroom with a brick floor that absorbs the heat during the day and releases it at night is another example. Even heating the water in a swimming pool in the sun is an example. When you build your home, you will want to take advantage of passive solar energy because it is a free gift from the sun.

Active solar energy uses mechanical devices in the collection, storage, and distribution of solar energy for your home. Active solar energy works by taking energy from the sun and, using solar panels, converts that energy into electricity. A component called an inverter works with the solar panels to convert the electricity from your panels into AC (alternating current) electricity. This electricity can be used right away or stored in a battery array in your home for future use.

There are five main components to a self-sustaining solar electric system:

1. Solar panels: may also be referred to as PV panels or modules. PV is short for photovoltaic ("light-powered"). A group of PV panels is called an array.

2. Mounting rack: metal support structures that hold an array of solar panels in a tilted position facing the sun. Some mounting racks can track the movement of the sun and shift the panels to collect as much energy as possible.

3. Charge controller: monitors and manages the electricity between the solar panels and the battery array.

4. Battery array or battery bank: a group of batteries wired together to capture the energy collected by the solar panels. These batteries can then be drawn on for electrical use.

5. Inverter: changes the battery power to AC power for everyday electrical use.

You will need to determine your power consumption before you can get started with any type of solar installation so you can choose the equipment that fits your needs.

DIG INTO GEOTHERMAL POWER

The word "geo" means earth and "thermal" means heat, so geothermal means heat from the earth. If you were to dig 10 feet below ground level, almost anywhere in the world, you would find the temperature to be between 50°F and 60°F (10°C and 16°C). No matter what the temperature outside, the readings 10 feet below the earth remain fairly constant. Geothermal heat pump systems use that constant temperature to either heat or cool your home. Using pipes that are buried in the ground near your home, fluid, such as antifreeze, is circulated through the heat pump system. In winter, heat from the warmer ground travels through the heat exchanger of the pump and sends warm air into your home. In summer, the cooler temperatures travel through the heat exchanger and cool the air in your home.

Geothermal heat pumps use much less energy than conventional heating systems because they draw heat from the ground and only have to potentially bring the temperature up several degrees. For example, with other heat sources, you have to maintain the fuel source to reach the internal home temperature of your choice. With geothermal, your heat source is already at 60°F and so only has to be heated another ten or so degrees to reach your comfort level. The same is true for air conditioning; the 60°F temperature can bring your home down to the level you desire without using excess energy. Geothermal heat systems can also heat your home's hot water.

Preserve Your Sustainable Lifestyle

To determine whether or not your location has enough sun or wind to supply energy, you can study maps at WindSolarEnergy.org (*www.windsolarenergy.org*) that show you how much solar or wind power you can expect. In some cases, you might need to use a combination in order be completely self-sustainable.

HARNESS HYDROELECTRIC POWER

Did you know that hydroelectric power is the most widely used renewable energy source in the world today? Worldwide, it accounts for approximately 16 percent of all electricity production. Much of the same technology used for massive hydroelectric plants can be used in powering your home.

Micro-hydro generators can use average water flows to generate electricity. The reason hydro power often surpasses solar and wind power in side-by-side comparisons is that water can generate power constantly, unlike sun and wind. If you've ever seen images of areas that have been flooded, you immediately understand the power of water.

Although most commercial hydroelectric power plants use a dam, for residential power generation you will typically use a pipe to collect water from a stream or river. The water from the pipes increases in power or energy as it flows downhill from the source to the turbine. The water hits the turbine and causes it to spin, which generates electricity.

 Self-Sufficient Facts, Knowledge, and Support
The force of water is so powerful that only 6" of water on a flooded street can cause you to lose control of your car. That same force, multiplied by four to equal 2 feet of water, can actually float your car downstream.

Before you can choose the correct hydro system for your home, you need to measure the amount of energy available in your water supply. To do this you need to determine two important numbers—flow and head. Hydroelectric installers will work with you to estimate these numbers, but you will want to have a general idea of how the process works.

The flow is the amount of water available to turn your turbine; the more flow, the more energy. Flow is measured in cubic feet per second. So, if you were to use a pipe to divert water from your source, how much would be diverted in one second?

Head is the pressure of the water when it hits the turbine. To determine head, you need to estimate the distance the water will fall (go downhill) before it reaches your turbine; the farther the fall, the higher the energy.

In order to use hydroelectric power efficiently, one or both of these numbers—flow or head—has to be fairly high to make the investment worth your while.

MAKE USE OF WIND POWER

Once you've found that your particular piece of property is appropriate for wind power, you should research the different costs of wind systems and which will meet your energy needs. Some are actually hybrid systems that include not only the wind system, but also solar panels and a generator to ensure an ample supply of power to your home.

A small self-sustaining wind system is actually quite simple. It generally consists of a wind turbine that generates electrical power, a battery bank that stores the power, and an inverter, which, just like the inverter in the solar power system, changes the power into usable electricity.

You need to place the wind turbine on a tower that is approximately 100 feet high. At this height the winds are generally faster and less turbulent. Two or three blades are attached to the turbine. When the wind blows over the blades, they rotate. When they rotate, a shaft inside the turbine converts that movement into electricity.

Smaller vertical wind turbines have recently been developed for use in home power. These turbines take up less space than traditional horizontal turbines, and some can capture wind movement from all directions.

A relatively new product on the wind-power market is a vertical spire. One such product, marketed as Windspire, generates power when wind blows against the vertical airfoils, causing them to spin. This power is then converted to AC electricity and is immediately available to provide energy to your building. These spires are only 30 feet tall and 4 feet wide. In 11 mph annual average winds, each spire will generate about 2,000 kWh per year.

CONSIDER WOOD-BURNING POWER

Humankind has been using wood for fuel ever since fire was discovered. Burning wood can be an inexpensive way to heat your home if you have a source for the wood you want to use. Does your land have several acres of hardwood? A good rule of thumb is that you need about ten acres of hardwood to produce enough wood to heat a home every year.

If you are able to cut, gather, and stack your own wood, you can really save money. The saying "when you cut your own wood, it heats you twice" is true. Harvesting wood is hard work, though, and caution must be maintained when using a chainsaw.

Self-Sufficient Facts, Knowledge, and Support
Biomass fuels, such as wood or corn, are "carbon neutral," which means they do not generate a net increase in greenhouse gas emissions. In fact, heating an average home with wood can save enough nonrenewable fossil fuel to operate an automobile for a full year.

If you have to have someone cut and deliver your wood, find out how much he or she charges. In some places, paying for wood is more expensive than using fossil fuels.

If you decide to use wood for heating, you have several output options: a fireplace, a wood stove, or a wood furnace.

Fireplaces

Using a fireplace is the most inefficient way to heat your home. Although charming, an open fireplace draws much more air than needed for combustion. This causes the warm air from the burning wood to be drawn up the chimney. Between 80 percent and 90 percent of the heat produced by wood burned in an open fireplace is lost up the chimney. The other drawback is that a fireplace will steal heated air from other parts of your home, because it will be drawing the air for combustion. This draw actually pulls cold air into your home through any unsealed areas, such as windows and doors.

If you have a home with an existing fireplace, you can purchase a fireplace insert that is designed to fit into your fireplace. An insert has a firebox that is surrounded by a steel shell. Air flows into the shell and radiant heat from the burning wood warms the air, which is then redistributed back into your home. This prevents the majority of the heat from escaping up the chimney and prevents the air draw in your home.

Wood Stoves

A wood stove is considered a "space heater" because, unlike a furnace that pushes heat through a duct system, it will heat a specific area in your home. New designs in wood stoves and tighter-built homes now make it possible to heat a home with a single wood stove. However, the stove needs to be centrally located so it can radiate heat throughout the area, and you must provide a way for heat to move through the rest of the home.

Wood stoves come in a variety of materials. Three of the most popular materials are cast iron, steel, and soapstone. Cast iron was the original material because the casting process was perfected long before steel and welding. You might even hear some people refer to wood stoves as "cast iron" stoves. The original Ben

Franklin stoves from the 1700s were cast iron. Steel-plated stoves are another choice. Steel stoves heat up quickly and start radiating heat faster than cast iron. But when the fire is reduced to coals, there is little or no residual radiated heat. On the other hand, a cast iron stove might take a few hours to start radiating heat, but when the fire is reduced to coals you will continue to have residual heat for several hours. Soapstone is a relatively soft metamorphic rock. It was used in early New England because residents found that not only could it be easily cut and polished, but it would also absorb the heat and then provide a gentle and steady radiant heat. You can stand near a soapstone stove without feeling overwhelmed by the heat, in comparison to a cast iron stove, which can overwhelm you with the force of the heat it generates.

CHAPTER 3

Growing Your Own Food

Having the ability to produce everything your family needs to stay healthy and active may sound like a daunting chore, but this part of a self-sufficient lifestyle isn't complicated. Even if you do everything wrong, you'll probably produce a sizable crop if you only make the effort. If you have never grown your own vegetables, then you need to brace yourself for what may be a life-altering experience. You are about to discover that even in your first, awkward attempts, you can grow food for yourself with superior flavor to the commercial products you've been eating all your life. Your produce may not be as flawless in appearance as that in the store, but because it has been allowed to grow naturally and ripen on the vine, you and your family will be able to appreciate the major differences in flavor, texture, and nutrition. More importantly, having an abundant crop of your own vegetables means fewer trips to the grocery store. It could even eliminate your dependence on commercial produce—an incredibly important step toward complete self-sufficiency. Natural, homegrown produce also ensures that the foods you're feeding your family are pesticide-free, leading to a healthier, safer lifestyle for your loved ones. Here are some notes and tips about how to cultivate and care for the most popular garden vegetables.

PLAN YOUR GARDEN

One of the most important parts of your garden is the planning. You can pour over seed catalogs all winter long to look for the seed varieties you'd like. You can meet with your agricultural extension agent, local farmers, or other self-sufficient homeowners to find out the particulars of gardening in your area. You can even meet with a master gardener who can answer many of your questions. But as you begin to plan your garden, you should ask yourself the following four questions.

Where Will Your Garden Be?

Generally, plants like lots of sun and well-drained soil. Look for places that are not shaded by trees or outbuildings. Try to find ground that is not rocky or sandy. Think about your water source. Is there a convenient way to transport water to your garden? How big do you want your garden to be? If you are planning to grow enough produce for your entire family, you should count on about 50 square feet of garden for each person, not counting paths.

How Will You Arrange Your Plants?

Are you going to use raised beds or use tilling? If you opt for raised beds, how are you going to place them? Are you going to plant single rows or double rows, or broadcast your seed over an area? How wide will your paths between rows be? If you use a rototiller or cultivator, you will want to plan your rows so it can easily be run up and down the paths. If you draw your garden on graphing paper, you can give each square a value—for example, each square is equal to 6 square inches—and plan your garden accordingly.

Preserve Your Sustainable Lifestyle

Raised bed gardening refers to gardening in soil that has been mounded or contained at a higher level than the surrounding soil. Raised bed gardening is an old gardening practice, but it's currently growing in popularity again because it offers several advantages over simply growing your plants in level ground. Raised bed gardens offer better protection from pests and garden path weeds; they provide excellent drainage and prevent erosion; and their warmth allows you to plant earlier in the season when the rest of the ground is still cold.

What Will You Plant?

Once you've decided where and how, deciding what to plant will help you with the placement of your plants. For example, if you are planting corn, you'll want to place it in an area where it won't shade other plants. If you are planting pumpkins or winter squash or watermelons, you'll want to plant them in an area where they have plenty of room to spread out. Companion plant by using flowers and herbs that discourage insects. Make the most out of your garden space by growing leafy vegetables that need partial shade, such as lettuce or chard, alongside semi-shading plants such as tomatoes. Plant what your family will eat. You might be able to get a bumper crop of radishes, but if your family won't eat them, they won't do you any good.

Self-Sufficient Facts, Knowledge, and Support
The USDA Hardiness Zone Map divides North America into eleven separate zones; each zone is 10°F warmer (or colder) in an average winter than the adjacent zone. If you see a hardiness zone in a catalog or plant description, chances are it refers to the USDA map.

When Should You Plant?

Your average local spring and fall frost dates are available from your county extension agent and online through most seed websites. When you pick out seeds, you should also take into account your climate zone, because that will show you how long your average growing season will be. For example, someone in North Carolina will have a longer growing season than someone in North Dakota. Some plants, such as peas and spinach, can be planted early in the spring; frost-tender plants, such as tomatoes and peppers, need to be started later in the season.

PREPARE YOUR LAND

To produce soil that yields the best garden, you should begin with a soil test. You can order a soil test from most online gardening sites or buy one at a local garden store. The test will measure the pH level of the soil as well as the amounts of nitrogen, phosphorus, and potash the soil contains. Each of these components plays an important role in the health of your garden:

- pH: Soil pH determines whether or not plants are able to consume nutrients. If the pH is too high or too low (too alkaline or too acidic), the nutrients in the soil cannot be absorbed into your plants.

- Nitrogen: Nitrogen produces the abundant growth of stalks, stems, leaves, and grasses. Too much nitrogen creates beautiful green plants with no fruit or seed formation. In other words, you would have beautiful-looking tomato plants with no tomatoes. Not enough nitrogen weakens plants, making them more susceptible to disease.

- Phosphorus: Phosphorus is necessary for the basic formation of the plant. It stimulates root formation, accelerates maturation, and promotes blooming and seed formation.

- Potash or Potassium: Potash stimulates early root or tuber formation, which is essential for vegetables such as carrots, potatoes, radishes, and peanuts. Too much potash diminishes a plant's resistance to weather extremes and postpones plant maturity.

Once you determine the nutrient needs of your soil, you should apply the proper fertilizer to meet those needs.

Tilling the soil before planting breaks up the ground, works fertilizer into the soil, and fights weeds. It allows the young sprouts of the seeds you plant to break through the soil. In addition, when you till in last year's leftover vines and stalks, you are adding what's called "green manure" to your garden and increasing the nutrients in your soil.

Another source of green manure is a cover crop, which is a crop planted specifically to be tilled into the soil. Usually green manure is planted in the fall, after your garden has been harvested. But you can also plant green manure on areas of your garden that are troubled with an influx of weeds. Cover crops help choke out weeds and leave the soil ready for planting. There are two types of green manure: legumes, such as alfalfa, clover, and soybeans, and nonlegumes, such as ryegrass, buckwheat, and oats. It's a good practice to use more than one kind of green manure and rotate your choices from year to year.

If you plant cover crops in the fall, till them into the ground in the spring before you begin to plant. If you plant cover crops during the spring to help choke out weeds, you can till the cover crops in just before you want to use the area for another crop.

Animal manure is another way to add nutrients to your soil. The most common types are cow, sheep, and chicken manure. You need to be sure that any manure you apply to your garden has aged at least six months to a year. You want to age manure for several reasons. First, fresh manure is "hot" (it has high levels of nitrogen) and it will burn your plants. Chicken manure especially is known for being hot and should be aged for a year. Also, fresh manure can carry bacteria that can cause illness. It also may have live weed seeds in it, especially if it's cow or sheep manure. Spreading this on your garden will be like planting weeds among your vegetables. Avoid manure from pigs, domestic animals such as dogs and cats, or humans. These all have a potential for carrying disease.

PLANT YOUR GARDEN

Now is the time to put all your planning to work. Using the garden layout you drew for your garden, place stakes to mark where different rows will be planted. The next step is to build trellises or string lines, or set in solid stakes, for any climbing plants such as peas, zucchini, or beans. In the area where you have dedicated space for your spreading plants, such as pumpkins and watermelons, build mounds several feet apart from each other, depending on the need of the specific plant variety. Be sure to create pathways right away, so you aren't tromping all over the garden and compacting the soil, and you won't inadvertently step on your seedbed.

The day before you plant, water your garden thoroughly. Start planting by reading the back of the seed packet to ensure you understand the planting depth and seed spacing. Seeds planted too deep or too close together will not do well. Be sure to place a marker at the end of each row with the name and variety of seed you have sown. If you change varieties in the middle of a row, place a marker there too.

Stretch a string between the two stakes you set to mark the row and create a V-shaped furrow with the corner of your hoe. Make sure the depth of the furrow corresponds to the planting depth recommended on the seed packet. Tear the corner of the seed package and carefully tap the package as you move down the row, dispensing the seeds evenly. Larger seeds can be placed individually in the row at the appropriate spacing. Plant some extra seeds in each row to allow for failed germination. You can thin these out later if needed.

When you cover the seeds, make sure the soil is fine, with no large clods or rocks. Pack the dirt lightly over the seeds. After you have finished planting all of the seeds in one section, water the garden thoroughly using a gentle spray so you soak the ground but don't disturb the seeds.

If you started your seeds indoors in pots and have bedding plants, you should follow the same steps you did with the seed sowing by stretching a string between the two stakes you set to mark the row. Using the string as a guide, dig small holes at the recommended spacing that are slightly wider and deeper than the root ball of the new plant. Water the plant thoroughly before setting it in the ground to lessen the shock of transplanting it. Holding the base of the plant with one hand, carefully maneuver the pot to loosen the roots and remove the new plant. Sometimes the roots may be compacted. Gently loosen the outer roots before you plant. Place the plant into the hole and pack the soil in around it, making certain that there is good soil/root contact.

Keep your garden watered to ensure good plant growth and germination. Once the seedlings emerge and develop their second or third set of true leaves, thin them so the strongest plants remain at the spacing directed on the seed package. Thinning early will prevent you from disturbing the roots of the remaining plants.

PLANT POTATOES

Potatoes originated high in the Andes of South America and are a cool-weather plant. Today, more potatoes are grown than any other vegetable. Potatoes benefit greatly from crop rotation, and they should never be planted in the same location in two successive years. Ideally, you'd plant them in an area that previously hosted a legume, and never following tomatoes, as they share many diseases. Potatoes require plenty of moisture and an acid soil. They like a fertile soil, but make certain that the plants don't come into contact with fresh manure or lime.

You can plant any potato for seed, but the best advice is that you only use certified seed stock; potatoes from the grocery store can carry disease, and may have been treated to keep from sprouting, which, of course, is what you want them to do.

Plant the seed potatoes 5" or 6" deep and about a foot apart. Being a cold-climate crop, potatoes like to stay cool, and this can be promoted by using a thick mulch of straw, leaves, or hay. Early varieties can be planted a week or two before the last frost of the season.

When the plants begin to make their tiny white flowers, you can dig them up for new potatoes. When the plants begin to wilt, they've grown as large as they're going to get, and they're ready to be dug up.

PLANT TOMATOES

Tomatoes are the most popular garden plant. Even if you have never grown any other plant, you can cultivate a few tomatoes in your backyard; they're easy to grow, prolific producers, and attractive to boot. There are literally hundreds of different tomato varieties in a rainbow of colors, including white, yellow, orange, purple, brown, black, and, of course, red. There are early and late varieties, low-acid and tangy varieties, slicing and paste varieties, and numerous other sorts. You'll have to determine which of these you like best through trial and error, but at this stage you only need to know about two different variations, and you can grow some of each if you like.

Choosing Tomatoes for Your Garden

First, you will choose whether to grow hybrid or heirloom varieties. Hybrids are known to have a robust vigor and may outproduce the heirloom varieties, but many of them have been developed for traits other than good taste: long shelf life, smooth, uncracked skin, compact growth habits, disease resistance, uniform shape for packing, and durability in shipping. Heirloom varieties, as the name suggests, are the strains that have been grown and handed down through generations. They may have lower yields and suffer more difficulties from insects or disease, but many people find their taste superior. The important thing is that you can save your heirloom seeds for planting next year, but seeds from your hybrids will not reproduce the same tomato that you grew the year before.

Self-Sufficient Facts, Knowledge, and Support
If the skin of your tomatoes is cracked, you may not be watering thoroughly enough. Instead of a quick sprinkle, give the soil a good soak once or twice a week so that the water goes deep and provides moisture evenly as the fruits form.

The second important distinction among tomatoes is between what are known as "determinate" and "indeterminate" varieties. Determinate tomatoes tend to bear their entire crop in a short period of time and grow on more manageable, compact vines, whereas the indeterminate varieties bear fruit over a longer period and grow on longer vines that require more staking. Obviously, the determinate varieties were developed with mass production in mind, where workers pick the fruit all at once and the more compact vines are somewhat easier to deal with in intensive planting. Unfortunately, this distinction is rarely noted when you're buying seeds or bedding plants, so you may need to do your own research to find out which you're getting.

Once you've decided which varieties you want to grow, if you're starting early enough, you can germinate your own seeds. If later, you'll have to buy commercial bedding plants, which may limit your choices.

Planting Tomato Seeds

To start seeds, set up a seedbed in a sunny south window in February or March, or about two months before the average last frost in your area. You can make your bed from fine, loose soil, or you may wish to start the seeds in peat pellets. Pellets do their job nicely and don't cause the transplanting shock that may come from using the soil bed. A cookie sheet with an outside lip of about ½" works nicely to contain your plants using either method. Tomatoes germinate best at about 70°F (21°C).

The seeds should begin to sprout within eight to ten days, and should be watered frequently from the bottom. This means you should pour the water into the container (cookie sheet) rather than directly on the seedlings. Let the soil surface remain dry, if possible, while keeping the soil around the seeds moist.

When the seedlings have developed three or four true leaves (not including the two small seed-leaves that form immediately after germination), transplant the sprouts to small containers, such as 8-ounce paper cups. Return them to the window. Check the seedlings daily, and don't let them start to droop from lack of water, but don't water them until they get soggy either.

When the sprouts are seven or eight weeks old, it's time to transplant them into the garden. Treat the starts as gently as you can, taking them out of their containers with as much soil clinging to the roots as possible. Plant them deep, burying them up to the first or second set of leaves, leaving the top shoot sticking out of the soil. Place the seedlings 12" to 18" apart.

If you follow these instructions, you'll be doing this around the date of the average last frost date in your area. That means it is very likely that it may frost after you've set out your plants. Cover them each night with frost protection, which is anything that amounts to a roof over the plants so that frost doesn't settle on the leaves. You'd need to remove the protection during the day, of course.

Tomatoes do very well grown in large tubs or in raised beds. In either case, however, they will need some support. A wire-mesh cage in a tubular shape works nicely. You place it over the plant, stake it down, and you're good to go. You can also press a post or stake 5 or 6 feet long into the soil and train the plant to grow upward by tying it to the stake, at intervals, with twist ties or scraps of cloth.

LOOK INTO SQUASH

The squash family consists of a diverse number of varieties, including pumpkin, zucchini, and spaghetti squash. Squash take up a lot of space, and don't produce a lot of fruit in return, especially the winter varieties. However, winter squash keep very well, and there's no denying the appeal of warm, buttered squash on a cold winter day. Provide your plants with a nice strong trellis they can grow on, to maximize the amount of fruit you can get in a small space. There are also bush varieties of squash, and this is a particularly rewarding route to take with popular summer varieties such as crooknecks.

Plant your seeds directly in the garden after all chance of frost has passed. Leave 2 feet between trailing varieties growing on a trellis. Bush varieties can be planted 16" to 24" apart, or one to a large container.

Squash self-prune their flowers. The plants will begin their blooming season by producing several of their typical large flowers, which will then fall off without producing fruit. This isn't a sign of something wrong. The plant generally produces female flowers before it produces any male flowers to pollinate them, so fruiting fails. Later in the year, when the plant has set a number of fruits and is working hard to develop them, it will prune off new fruits before they begin to mature and use up resources.

Self-Sufficient Facts, Knowledge, and Support

Squash beetles suck the sap from winter squash and pumpkins in a very destructive manner. If you see a squash beetle, kill it immediately and look for more. Then look for clusters of small, round eggs on the underside of the leaves. Remove the eggs with the sticky side of duct tape and destroy them.

CHECK OUT CORN

Corn is one of the only native American vegetables; it has been grown in North America for more than 4,000 years. Corn takes a lot of nitrogen out of the soil, so you should fertilize it heavily with compost. Plant your corn in the same bed as your squash and beans. The beans will provide nitrogen for the corn, the corn will provide stalks for the beans to climb up, and the squash will create living mulch, covering the ground to keep weeds from sprouting.

Plant corn seed about 2" deep and thin so that you wind up with a plant about every 12". Corn likes heat and it likes water, two things that seem at odds with one another. Plant corn two weeks after your last frost date, when the soil is at least 60°F (16°C). A good strategy is to apply thick mulch, even if you grow the corn with squash, to hold in the moisture. Because the sugar in corn deteriorates rapidly after the ears are picked, many gardeners like to plant corn in successive plantings so that they never have too much at one time. Corn is pollinated by the wind, so plant your corn in blocks rather than in long rows.

PLANT PEAS AND BEANS

Beans and peas are legumes, which means that they "fix" nitrogen in the soil. This has little effect when the plants are growing, but after they've died, the soil they leave behind will be richer in nitrogen—a fact you should consider when arranging your rotation-planting schedule.

Peas may be planted very early in the year, four to six weeks before the last frost is expected. Plant the seeds about 1" deep, and sprinkle some wood ashes left over from a wood fire over the soil if you have them available. Peas like a humus-rich, well-drained soil. Peas seem impervious to cold. It isn't at all unusual to see them growing while covered with snow. Peas aren't fond of warm weather (over 70°F, 21°C), and you're more likely to endanger your crop by putting it in too late than too early.

Beans require warmer weather. Don't try starting bean seeds indoors, as they don't transplant well; wait until after frost and plant the seeds 1" deep. Beans come in two varieties: pole and bush beans. Bush beans have a compact, bushy habit that allows them to spread to 2 feet in diameter, but they don't need staking. Pole beans, on the other hand, need stakes or poles to climb to keep them off the ground. Beans respond well to heavy mulching and regular soil. You can pick beans all summer long if you plant them in two-week succession plantings.

Peppers, both hot and sweet, come in many shapes and colors. They grow on a bushy, attractive plant—some varieties are grown specifically as ornamental plants, so if you want to place a few alongside the front walk, they'll look very nice. They are grown as annuals, but are actually perennials. If you bring some indoors after frost, they will continue to bear fruit for a while

Self-Sufficient Facts, Knowledge, and Support
Both sweet peppers and chili peppers are excellent sources of vitamin C. In fact, according to Healthaliciousness.com, green chili peppers provide more vitamin C than any other food, with 242.5 milligrams per 100-gram serving. That's 404 percent of the vitamin C your body needs each day, from just one serving.

Start your seeds indoors eight to ten weeks before you plan to transplant them to the garden. You can follow the same procedure as with planting tomatoes, but only plant the seedlings as deep as they grow as sprouts. Peppers also do well in containers, and their compact, bushy nature makes them easy to arrange in beds, where you should plant them 18" apart. Pepper plants have few natural enemies; the hot varieties have even fewer still. In fact, you can use a purée of the seeds of hot peppers, along with soap, to make an organic insect repellant. If you have a problem with marauding deer, the compact growth habit of pepper plants makes them ideal to fit into cages.

LOOK INTO LETTUCE

One of the easiest and earliest gardens you can grow is a salad garden of green leafy vegetables. Start with leaf lettuce and expand from there to head lettuce, spinach, chard, and other greens. Leaf lettuce is among the easiest of all garden plants to cultivate. If you can keep the plants from getting too hot and dry in summer, you can grow successive plantings that will keep you in salad makings from frost to frost.

Sow your lettuce seeds directly into the garden, in fine soil, as early in spring as you can work the ground. Keep the seeds moist, and they should germinate in about a week. Sowing lettuce seeds is rather tricky. They are very small, and it's difficult not to wind up planting them too densely. At any rate, plant them about ¼" deep, and when the sprouts start showing themselves, thin them to about one every 3" or 4". Later, you'll want to thin them again to about 10" apart. In all likelihood, this will be the first crop you'll get from your garden, and will be tastier and more tender than what you get at the grocery store. You'll be full of pride.

Self-Sufficient Facts, Knowledge, and Support
You can get detailed information on the projected first and last frost dates in your area by looking up the National Climatic Data Center website online at *www.ncdc.noaa.gov*. It provides frost probability data for spring and fall at every weather station in your state.

Like most leafy greens, lettuce is a cool-weather plant, and it doesn't react well to heat. You can have a summer crop and a fall crop, but you may have a bit of trouble keeping the plants from drying out in July or August.

CULTIVATE THE BRASSICAS VEGETABLES

Although they may look quite dissimilar, cabbage, broccoli, cauliflower, and Brussels sprouts are closely related, and their cultivation is pretty similar as well. They all like cool weather, and you're best advised to get them in the ground as soon as possible. Unfortunately, this means planting started plants as early as you can to avoid frost exposure (although they can withstand light frosts). If it remains cool in your area long enough, you can make successive plantings as the season progresses. The immature plants are almost identical, but cauliflower is the most difficult of the group to grow. For an intensive planting, space the plants about 12" apart and sow seeds 1" deep.

 Self-Sufficient Facts, Knowledge, and Support
You can "blanch" plants you want to keep light-colored, such as cauliflower, by pulling the leaves over the growing head and tying them there. As a word of caution, this can cause rainwater to bead and set on the head, which may cause rot if you allow an opening in the leaves.

You may find out that brassicas do better in your area planted for the fall season.

MAKE SPACE FOR HERBS

Humankind has been using herbs for myriad purposes throughout recorded history, and small wonder, for they are easy to grow, are prolific, and have so many uses in the home and on the farm.

Growing herbs in containers is an easy decision to make, because they grow well in small spaces. They grow well in larger spaces, too, so keeping them contained also protects the rest of the garden from being overrun. On the other hand, because so many herbs are beneficial to so many plants, tucking them into unused corners of your beds can provide insect protection to your other cultivars. In general, basil, borage, marigold, and nasturtium are helpful herbs that you should have scattered around the garden all summer long.

Using containers to grow herbs allows you flexibility that is not available when herbs are grown in the ground. For example, during the summer months when frequently used kitchen herbs such as fresh basil or chives are in high demand—and at peak production— you may want to move a few of those containers close to the kitchen door for a while. Later you can move them back to the garden for over-wintering. Also, beneficial flowers can be propagated in containers in the garden and moved to the front lawn during their blooming period to the benefit of your lawn plants and the enjoyment of your guests.

CONSIDER FRUIT TREES

Fruit trees need full sun for proper growth and quality fruit production. When looking at a site for an orchard, seek land that has good water drainage and does not lie low in the terrain. Low areas are often frost pockets, because cold air settles into low areas, and the flowers on the fruit trees are very susceptible to a late freeze.

The early morning sun is particularly important because it dries the dew from the leaves, thereby reducing the incidence of diseases. Fruit planting sites should have good air circulation. Fruit trees grow well in a wide range of soil types. They prefer soils with a texture of sandy loam to a sandy clay loam. Ideal soil pH for fruit trees is 6.5.

What Size Trees Should You Choose?

The common sizes available for fruit trees are dwarf, semi-dwarf, and standard. The size you choose depends on how long you want to wait for your first harvest, how much space you have for your orchard, and how much you want your harvest to yield.

Dwarf

Dwarf fruit trees can flourish in an 8-foot-diameter plot. Because of their size, they are easy to prune and harvest. However, even given their smaller stature, the fruit is normal size. Dwarf trees are not as hardy as standard or semi-dwarf trees, partly because they have fairly shallow roots, so a hard frost can kill them. For this reason, dwarf trees should not be grown in USDA zones 3 or 4.

You should plant dwarf trees at least 8 feet apart, but no farther than 20 feet apart to ensure pollination. They should also be staked because of their lack of root depth. Dwarf trees can produce one to two bushels a year in about two years, and they will live about fifteen to twenty years.

Semi-Dwarf

Semi-dwarf are medium-sized trees that require a growing area of about 15 feet in diameter. They need annual pruning to keep the height down and the shape balanced. They are sometimes called semi-vigorous. Semi-dwarf apple trees will grow about 15 to 20 feet tall. They are hardier than dwarf trees, but still not as hardy as standard trees and should not be grown in USDA zone 3. Semi-dwarf trees should be planted at least 10 to 20 feet apart. However, in order to ensure pollination, do not plant them more than 20 feet away from another variety. A good semi-dwarf tree should live about twenty to twenty-five years and produce about five bushels of apples per year within three to four years.

Standard

If you have an older fruit tree on your property, it probably is a standard. Standard apple trees will grow about 25 feet tall, and even taller if they are never pruned. Standards were the only choice before the smaller hybrids were developed. They are hardiest and will adapt to a variety of soils and climates. Standard trees should be planted about 25 to 30 feet apart. However, do not plant them more than that distance from another variety in order to ensure pollination. A standard tree should live fifty years or longer and produce about eight bushels of apples a year within five to six years.

Consider Your Planting Zone

Which varieties do best in your planting zone? You can ask your county extension agent, the nursery owner, or your neighbors to see which trees have produced the best fruit for them. Determine whether you have a microclimate, a small area that differs from your general climate zone, on your property where warmer-zone trees might thrive.

Determining Ideal Soil

You need to match the kind of tree you want to the kind of soil you have. Some fruit trees, such as plums, do well in damp soil conditions. Other fruit trees, such as apples, need well-drained soil. Some varieties might be more drought resistant than others, or more frost resistant. When you meet with your local nursery, garden center, or county extension agent, describe the area you have in mind as your orchard location and ask an expert to help you pick out trees that would grow best in that location.

Pollination Essentials

Make sure, if needed, to provide pollinators for your trees. Some trees, such as most varieties of peaches and nectarines, are self-pollinating, but others, such as apricot trees, require another tree of the same type for pollination. Be sure that you match your tree with the correct pollinator. Just because you have two apple trees does not mean they are pollinators for each other. Check with either your extension agent or the nursery where you purchase your trees to be sure you have the right varieties.

Planting Your Fruit Tree

Once you have decided the size tree you want and your soil type, it is time to plant your fruit tree. Soak the tree roots before planting. Dig a hole that is about 10" wider than the size of the root ball of the tree and deep enough to completely cover the roots. Be sure the graft union or graft line of the tree lies slightly above the level of the ground. The graft line can be identified as a diagonal scar on the trunk or as a lump a few inches above the soil level mark on the tree.

After digging, loosen the soil around the hole so that the tree can easily expand its roots. Put some soil at the bottom of the hole in order to make a mound in the center. Carefully place the root ball of the tree on top of the mound. After placing the tree in the hole, fill it with soil. Gently firm the soil around the tree and then water to settle the soil around the roots. Apply a layer of mulch or organic material, such as compost or leaves, around the base of the tree to help retain moisture—do not place the material near the graft line of the tree.

Check with your local nursery or county extension agent to find out when fruit trees should be planted in your area.

PLANT SOME BERRY BUSHES

It's a good idea to have several varieties of berries in your garden, as well as a thriving fruit orchard. Strawberries will bear in June, raspberries and blueberries in July, and blackberries in August and September. You can have fresh berries all summer long!

Strawberries
Plant your strawberries in a sunny location for the sweetest berries and the healthiest plants. If you have a spot on a south-facing slope, that would be ideal. Strawberry plants are usually planted in early spring in the north, but in the south, the fall works best. Strawberries love fertile, slightly acidic well-drained soil. If your soil is a heavy clay, you might want to consider raised beds for your berries.

Select plant varieties that do well in your area. Ask your local extension agent or a good local strawberry grower which ones do best. Strawberries come in two basic types: June-bearing and everbearing. Plant varieties of each to extend your harvest. Strawberry plants are usually sold in bunches of twenty-five, and one or two bunches will be enough if you are starting a bed.

Plant as early as you can and only use dormant plants. Soak roots in water as your make a furrow in the row where the strawberries will be planted. Plant in rows 4 feet apart. Trim roots so they are 4" to 5" long. Put some soil at the bottom of the row in order to make a mound in the center. Carefully place the trimmed roots over the mound of soil and then add soil on top of the roots. Be sure the base of the crown is just at the soil surface. Firm the soil around the plant and water well.

Mulch and fertilize your strawberries. During the first season, do not allow your plants to produce fruit; pinch off all the blossoms. This will allow the plants to put their energy into developing runners. Be sure to protect your strawberries in the winter. A 6" layer of straw over the plants will help insulate them from the freezing and thawing cycles.

Blueberries

Blueberries prefer full sunlight and grow best in well-drained, sandy soils rich in organic matter with a soil pH of 4 to 4.5. When planting, dig a hole 18" deep and 18" wide. Mix equal amounts of peat moss with topsoil and pour into the hole until it is filled 4" from the top. Set the plant and cover the roots with the remaining peat-soil mix.

Space plants 5 feet apart in rows 10 feet apart. Apply 4" of sawdust or wood-chip mulch in a 2-foot-wide band after planting. Beginning the next year, maintain a 4" mulch depth in a 4-foot band over the life of the planting.

Blueberry bushes need at least 1" to 2" of water per week. In dry seasons, supplemental watering is essential to obtain good yields of high-quality fruits. Once you reach early fall, however, do not apply extra water unless the soil is very dry.

Self-Sufficient Facts, Knowledge, and Support
Blueberries contain significant quantities of both anti-bacterial and antiviral compounds and have a reputation in northern Europe of fighting infections. They may also help protect against heart disease.

Remove blossoms that appear in the first year of planting and second year after planting to stimulate vigorous growth.

Raspberries and Blackberries

Bramble berries prefer full sunlight and grow best in well-drained, sandy loam soils rich in organic matter. Berries prefer a soil pH of 5.6 to 6.2. Avoid low areas that remain wet late into the spring. However, you should ensure that the plants receive plenty of water during dry periods.

You should also be aware of what was planted prior to putting in the brambles. Certain vegetables such as tomatoes, potatoes, peppers, and eggplants carry a fungus called *Verticillium*. This fungus lives in the soil for four to six years and attacks plants from their roots. Brambles are highly susceptible to *Verticillium*.

You will want to plant your brambles in the early spring, but wait until any danger of frost has passed. When you are planting the individual canes, be sure to keep them moist during the process. Dig a small hole; it should be large enough for the roots to spread out, but not so large that the plants would be set deeper than they were in the nursery.

Make sure the soil around both the roots and the plant is firm. Then generously water each plant.

CHAPTER 4

Raising Animals

Raising your own animals for food sources and for profit can be an immensely rewarding experience. And, if you decide to grow crops and raise animals simultaneously, your crops will nurture your livestock, and your livestock will nurture your crops. However, raising animals can be one of the most challenging aspects of a self-sufficient lifestyle, so it is incredibly important that you recognize how much planning, work, and effort go into this process.

It is difficult to make money raising livestock of any sort. Animals need to be fed regularly, which can expand your cost of operations and deflate your budget. In addition to that, many laws regulate the sale of milk and meat, which may make selling those items impractical for the small farmer. Then there are the veterinary bills.

These challenges can be worth the work because you'll have access to higher-quality meats than you can buy in the store. As your experience and capabilities grow, you're likely to find more ways to cut costs and increase profits, but you should expect to fall short of breakeven as a beginner. Read on to learn the best ways for raising animals in your new self-sufficient lifestyle.

RAISE RELIABLE COMPANIONS

Cats and dogs are more than just friendly pets to the self-sufficient homeowner. They also provide protection for your livestock and crops, your farm and home, and your family members too. If you plan to raise your own animals, be sure to research the best dog breeds for herding and protection purposes. It would also behoove you to keep some healthy barn cats around too, to ensure the heath of your livestock—these expert hunters keeps rodents and pests at bay, protecting your animals from sickness and disease.

Get a Dog

A dog will not only provide companionship, but he will also provide protection for you, your family, and your livestock. If you already have a dog as part of your family, remember that switching to a self-sufficient lifestyle may be a culture shock for him too. Don't let your dog run loose; he may not be able to find his way home. And, if you move to a new property that is close to farmers with livestock, be sure to keep your dog on your property until you've had a chance to introduce him to your neighbors. Some farmers have no qualms about shooting an unknown dog that wanders close to their property.

Self-Sufficient Facts, Knowledge, and Support

Dogs are descended from a small, weasel-like mammal called Miacis, which was a tree-dwelling creature that existed about 40 million years ago. The domestic dog of today first appeared in Eurasia about 13,000 years ago, and was probably a direct descendant of a small, gray wolf.

Dogs, like people, have their own unique temperaments, but certain breeds are more suited to living on a farm than others. These breeds, which tend to be the herding dogs and the working dogs, somehow understand that your chickens are not playthings, but are part of their pack and need to be protected. However, even these breeds need to be trained properly to respect the other livestock and understand that you and your family members are the alphas in his pack, which means you need to be obeyed. Here is a list of dog breeds recommended for farms:

- Border collie is one of several herding breeds popular as farm dogs. Weighing between 27 and 45 pounds, the border collie is a medium-sized dog with high energy. Border collies are very smart and easy to train, but they need lots of activity to keep them happy.
- Scotch collie is also known as the farm collie or old farm collie. The Scotch collie is larger than the border collie and not quite as energetic, but is devoted to its master and delighted to do his bidding.
- Australian shepherd is another herding breed popular for farms. Also known as Aussies, they are natural herders as well as good watchdogs. They are medium-sized dogs with friendly dispositions, and they interact well with children and other dogs.
- Australian cattle dog is also called a blue heeler. They are smart and easily trained. Because they are territorial, they are good watchdogs, but they have a hard time sharing their territory with other animals.
- Corgis are small herding dogs that are good farm dogs. Their bodies are similar to medium-sized dogs, but their extremely short legs classify them as small herding dogs. They are

intelligent and very energetic. They were originally bred to drive cattle, hunt vermin, and guard farms in the United Kingdom. Because of its close-to-the-ground stature, the corgi herds by barking and nipping at the heels of livestock.

■ German shepherds, although often used as guard dogs, are actually a herding breed. German shepherds are loyal and intelligent and can be trained as sheepdogs. Full grown, they can weigh between 75 and 85 pounds.

■ Bernese mountain dog is a large working breed. These dogs were bred to guard sheep in the Swiss Alps, and also to pull milk carts. They warned of intruders but were not aggressive because they lived with the animals they protected. They grow to be 80 to 100 pounds and, because of their heavy coats, may not be suited to warmer climates.

■ Great Pyrenees is a nonherding dog well suited for life in colder climates. Like its cousin, the Bernese mountain dog, the Great Pyrenees was bred to protect flocks of sheep and goats. It is considered to be a guardian of family, farm, and livestock. Calm and loyal, this breed is also fiercely independent, which can create problems while training.

■ Old English sheepdog is another herding breed popular on farms. Appearing in movies such as *The Shaggy Dog* and *Peter Pan*, its family-friendly temperament is well known. Old English sheepdogs herd by bumping rather than nipping— and with an average weight of 60 to 100 pounds, when they bump you, you feel it.

Ultimately, the breed of dog you choose will make a significant impact on your home and farm. Man's best friend will prove to be a loyal companion and protector to you, your family, and your livestock.

Rely on Barn Cats

One of the most natural ways to prevent rodent infestation and keep the population of other small animals such as rabbits and snakes to a minimum is to have some barn cats. Barn cats are not spoiled lap cats. They are usually at least partly feral cats who take the role of hunter and protector seriously.

You might have already inherited barn cats when you purchased your property. If not, ask around; someone is usually in need of a home for some new barn kittens.

Although these are not pets, you have a responsibility to care for them just like any other animal on your property. Here are some of the things you should consider to ensure that you have healthy and helpful barn cats:

Deworming

Because the main job of your barn cats is to catch and kill mice, they are susceptible to transmission of the worms that reside inside the rodents. Your veterinarian can prescribe a broad spectrum dewormer. Ask your veterinarian how often you should administer the medicine to your cat.

Heartworms are carried by mosquitoes, so if you live in an area where mosquitoes are plentiful, you will want to give your barn cat a monthly heartworm preventive. Be sure to have your cat tested before you begin preventative measures, because if your cat already has heartworms, they must be eliminated from the cat's system first.

Vaccination for Feline Diseases

A number of diseases are considered the "core" cat diseases: feline herpes virus, calicivirus, and panleukopenia (distemper) virus. Your veterinarian can give your cat a combination vaccination when the cat is still young and then annually to continue protection. Rabies virus vaccine is also necessary for your barn cat, especially if there are bats that are infected with rabies in your area. Rabies-infected bats eventually become paralyzed and fall to the ground. Before they die, they twitch around, and could attract the attention of your barn cat.

FeLV/FIV Testing and Vaccination

Feline leukemia, or feline immunodeficiency virus, is the equivalent of HIV in cats. If your veterinarian performs a simple blood test on your cat, she will be able to determine whether your cat is a carrier. Many cats with FeLV/FIV do fine, but about one-third become very ill and can transfer the disease to other cats. If your barn cat has FeLV/FIV, you will want to vaccinate the uninfected cats so they don't become sick.

Self-Sufficient Facts, Knowledge, and Support

Antifreeze poisoning is fatal in cats and dogs, if left untreated. Unfortunately, antifreeze also tastes good to these animals. In addition, you need to be sure that chemicals, pesticides, insecticides, rat poison, and even moldy feed are disposed of in closed containers where your animals cannot gain access to them.

Nutrition

Just because your barn cat catches mice, rabbits, and even squirrels does not mean that it doesn't need a supplemental diet. You want to maintain a healthy barn cat, and a good-quality dry diet is all your cat requires. Keep a bowl full of dry food and another bowl filled with fresh water for your cats.

Check on Your Barn Cats

Barn cats will usually remain healthy if they have high-quality food and clean water. But when cats become ill, they often try to hide it. Barn cats will usually greet you as you go about your morning chores, but you should do a quick check of your cats at least once a week to see if you notice any signs of illness. If you suspect something, call your local veterinarian and explain the problem to her. She will be able to explain your options for treatment.

TAKE CARE OF SMALL LIVESTOCK

If you're just starting to raise your own animals, an investment in small livestock is a great one to make. Not only are the smaller animals easier to handle, but they also require less space than their larger livestock counterparts. Sheep, goats, and rabbits can still provide the milk, wool, fur, manure, and meat you need, without sacrificing huge acres of land and large sums of cash.

Raise Sheep

Sheep have been domesticated longer than any other animal except the dog—more than 110 centuries—so it's no surprise that there are so many breeds and so many uses for sheep. Sheep are raised for meat, wool, milk, leather, and, in recent years, as eco-friendly lawnmowers. Sheep differ from goats in a number of ways, but diet and temperament are most important to the inexperienced farmer. Goats will eat leaves, brush, shrubs, and vines, whereas sheep prefer a pasture of soft flowering plants and grasses. Sheep are also easier to keep behind a fence than the more gregarious goats.

If your self-sufficient home lies on a small plot of land, you may have some difficulty finding a financial rationalization for adding the term "shepherd" to your resume. As with any other meat animal, it's hard to match the price of lamb or mutton in the store to raising your own. Of course, in addition to the meat, sheep can give you wool, but unless you do some creative marketing, what the commercial market will pay for wool doesn't make it worth your effort. It's best to use your wool for your own needs at home.

Even though people have been milking sheep for millennia, virtually no one consumes sheep's milk in its fresh state. Instead, this milk goes into some of the finest cheeses in the world. Owing in part to how long sheep have been domesticated, there are hundreds of individual breeds of sheep, and each of them has particular uses. A few of these are as follows:

A SAMPLING OF SHEEP BREEDS BY USE		
Meat	Wool	Milk
Coolalee	Bond	British Milksheep
Dorper	Romney	East Friesian
Dorset	Rambouillet	Lacaune
Llanwenog	Lleyn	Latxa
Polled Dorset	Navajo-Churro	Sardinian

Of course, there are also numerous breeds that claim to be good for more than one use.

Sheep Housing and Fencing

The sort of housing you'll need for your flock depends a lot on the usual variables: your climate and your available cash.

Assuming you have a reasonably moderate climate and not a lot of available cash, you can probably serve your charges well with a three-sided shed with an open side facing south. About 10 square feet per sheep will be about the right size, but of course more is always better.

There are two popular fencing solutions to keep sheep in and predators out. The traditional fence is 48"-high woven wire with a strand of barbed wire or electric wire above it. Woven wire is quite expensive. The modern, cheaper solution is an electric fence made up of six or seven strands of electric wire with decreasing space between the strands the lower they are installed on the fence.

A good pasture for sheep will consist of cool-season grasses and legumes.

Get Some Goats

Goats and sheep have their similarities, of course, but their personalities are very different. Goats are an excellent choice for a smaller self-sufficient home. They're more popular than sheep, possibly because they are seen more as milk animals than meat providers, although they are, of course, both. Goats also are noted producers of marketable hair, called cashmere in this case, which is a fine, downy undercoat of hair that grows as the autumn days grow shorter in length.

Milking goats should be fed high-quality hay, either grass or legume, and a grain ration that will support their health and milk production. Lactating does should have all the hay they will eat, plus a pound of grain for each three pounds of milk they produce. Sweet feed for milk cows will serve goats as well.

If you've ever seen a mountain goat scrambling across the rocky face of a precipice, then you can imagine how their domesticated cousins may be a bit difficult to keep behind a fence. You can lessen this problem a bit by providing your goat with company, as goats are quite outgoing and enjoy the presence of other goats.

A SAMPLING OF GOAT BREEDS BY USE			
Meat	Fiber	Milk	Dual purpose
Auckland Island	Australian Cashmere	Anglo-Nubian	Pyrenean
Barbari	Canindé	American Lamancha	Chamoisee
Rove	Pygora	British Alpine	Sahelian

Goat Housing and Fencing

Goats do not like getting wet one little bit. As with sheep, a three-sided shed with the open side facing south will make a good shelter, except in extremely cold climates. The roof must withstand goat traffic, because if goats can climb on it, they will. Goats are also more curious and adventuresome than sheep, which is not necessarily a good thing if you're the one responsible for keeping them penned in.

There is no goat-proof fence, but a reasonable attempt at goat fencing would be five-foot-high woven wire with fairly close openings, such as a 2" × 4" mesh. Be sure you use woven wire rather than welded wire. The emphasis is usually on fencing the goats into their pasture, but if you live in the country, or even close to it, your greater concern may be fencing out predators. If so, you'll discover that it takes a pretty good fence to keep a coyote away from a flock of tasty goats or sheep, so a good additional measure you can take is to acquire a good guard dog.

Livestock Guardian Dogs (LGD) are usually bonded to the herd as puppies and they function as members of the flock. They may blend in with the ruminants, as many are the same colors as "their" sheep or goats. These breeds have an instinctual desire to guard the flock, and their mere presence is usually enough to keep predators at a respectful distance.

Self-Sufficient Facts, Knowledge, and Support
Doesn't goat's milk have a funny sort of "goaty" taste? It can, but shouldn't. Milk from a lactating doe kept in close proximity to a buck or one fed on certain plants (brassicas and alliums) near milking time can have an unpleasant flavor, but these situations are easily avoided.

Rear Rabbits

It is unlikely that you'll find a cheaper, easier, more efficient way to produce meat than raising rabbits. Their requirements are so minimal that almost anyone can raise them and get started right away. Rabbits are raised commercially for meat and fur, and more than a few gardeners raise bunnies exclusively to get the benefits of their manure, which is a boon to any compost pile.

Rabbits are typically raised for two purposes: for meat and as show animals. It is worth noting that although rabbits are easy, fun, and reasonably inexpensive to raise, they are not particularly profitable from a financial standpoint. Rabbits can provide you with a source of high-quality meat with a very low cholesterol content and high digestibility, but there isn't a large market for the meat.

The two most popular rabbit breeds raised for meat are the Californian and the New Zealand White. A good starting point for the novice would be to purchase a young buck and three or four young does. This gives them the time to acclimate themselves to their surroundings before they begin breeding.

Rabbit Housing

Some breeders raise rabbits on rotating pasture, but rabbits appear to be perfectly happy living out their lives in cages. An individual cage, or hutch, can be 24" × 30" and tall enough for the largest of them to stand up, with a little more room given to does with litters. Because the bunnies will tolerate such close quarters, giving them just the right environment is a very easy thing to do. They are most sensitive to heat (high temperatures can prove fatal), so the hutch should be kept in a cool, shady, and well-ventilated place—ideally on the north side of a building or fence—in the summer months; in winter, they can be moved either to the south side of the building or taken inside a barn or shed.

Your rabbits will require plenty of water and will do very well on commercial rabbit pellets, which you may wish to augment with grass, clover, alfalfa, and other forages.

Make Money Off Alpacas

Alpacas are related to llamas, vicunas, and camels. They originated in South America, where they have been domesticated for millennia for their fiber and meat. Alpacas have been imported to the United States since 1983. Registered animals tend to command a high price, even today, largely because the Alpaca Registry Inc. only permits registration of the offspring of currently registered animals, thus eliminating competition from animals imported from Peru or Bolivia. Full-grown adults are about 3 feet tall at the withers and weigh around 150 pounds. A baby alpaca is called a "cria." Adults usually produce one cria per year. Alpacas have a gentle, even disposition, but have been known to kick and spit, mostly at other alpacas, but occasionally at humans.

Raising these animals doesn't have any complex requirements. Housing and fencing that work for sheep will work as well for alpacas (they're also ruminants), and sheep pasture plus some low-protein grass hay will provide their diet. It is claimed that alpacas eat far less than most animals of their size.

There are two basic types of alpaca: Huacaya and Suri. Huacaya have more compact bodies and fiber similar to sheep's wool, whereas the Suri exhibit longer necks and legs, are generally lankier, and their fiber is similar to that of lustrous hair.

Alpacas are initially quite expensive, and the self-sufficient farmer who wants to raise them needs to either raise and breed them for show and, thus, for the sale of equally expensive offspring, or get cheap pet-quality individuals for fiber collection. If you're only casually interested in these animals, you'd do better to look at more common livestock unless you are willing to become deeply committed financially.

CONSIDER LARGE LIVESTOCK

If you're ready to take on the challenge of raising large livestock, be sure to read the following sections carefully. Larger livestock take up more room on your farm, require more feed and attention than smaller animals, and can cause serious damage to your property if not properly penned in and cared for. This ultimately requires more of your time, money, and effort, but the rewards of caring for larger animals translate into more products (milk, meat, fiber, manure) for your family to use and for your farm to sell.

Look Into Miniature Cattle

Small cattle are relatively new animals on the scene. As of this book's publication, the International Miniature Cattle Breeders Society and Registry lists twenty-six breeds of compact cattle, most of which you would recognize as smaller versions of common cattle breeds, from Angus to Zebu.

Self-Sufficient Facts, Knowledge, and Support
Most cows require more effort to milk than goats, and most miniature milk cows' udders are too close to the ground for comfortable milking. This can be remedied by building a platform for the miniature cow to stand on, raising her udders for milking.

The mini-cattle business is still in its infancy. Like all new breeds, most of the examples you'll find for sale are quite expensive, and their owners treat them more like pets than livestock. The best way to make money in miniature cattle, at this time at least, is to breed them for sale as registered purebreds. They are quite acceptable as beef or dairy animals, but until the prices begin to drop, these little animals will make for some very expensive beef and/or milk. So if it's food you're looking for, you might be better off with goats or sheep, but if you can afford the initial price, you stand to make more money raising miniature cattle for resale.

MINIATURE CATTLE BREEDS	
Breed	Full-Sized Counterpart
American Beltie	Belted Galloway
Dexter	N/A
Highland Miniature	Scottish Highland
Lowline Angus	Aberdeen Angus
Miniature Hereford	Hereford
Miniature Jersey	Jersey
Miniature Zebu	Zebu
Panda	N/A
Red Kentshire	Dexter/Hereford cross

Miniature Cattle Housing and Fencing

If you have experience with full-sized cattle, you only need to downsize from that to get the mini-cattle equivalent. A three-sided loafing shed is plenty of shelter, and your tiny cattle will use about one-third the pasture area you'd need for standard cattle.

Miniature cattle range in size from around 36" to 46" at the shoulder, so the barbed-wire fence that you'd use for large cattle will work fine and can be a foot or so lower in height. This brings up one of the most practical aspects of raising miniature cattle. If you've ever had to load a 1,500-pound steer into a truck or catch and restrain him for veterinary work, you'll immediately appreciate the convenience of dealing with animals that top out at around half that weight. Not only are you less likely to suffer pain and injury to your person, but mini-cows put less stress on the facilities as well, and fences, pastures, and equipment don't require so much upkeep as they do when you're raising full-sized bovines.

Preserve Your Sustainable Lifestyle
If you plan to keep livestock, remember that your animals will need your attention every day. You must make certain that they are fed and watered and that their living quarters are clean and dry. If you take frequent spur-of-the-moment vacations, you'll need to find someone to care for your animals while you're gone.

Purchase Some Pigs

The two major considerations you have when raising pigs are (1) whether you are going to buy feeders (young pigs that have been weaned and weigh about 40 pounds) or raise them yourself from your own litter, and (2) site selection.

When you purchase your pigs, look for the cream of the crop; they should be healthy and in good condition when purchased. Characteristics to look for include smooth hair coat, pink skin color, and alertness. Don't buy the runt no matter what kind of "deal" you can get for it. Runts don't have a good feed-to-flesh conversion ratio, and you will be tossing good money after bad. If you are simply raising a pig for meat, it will take from five to seven months to bring it up to the 200-pound mark, which is the optimal weight for a pig. When it gets much bigger than 200–220 pounds, you decrease efficiency (it takes more feed per pound of gain) and you increase the fat. You will obtain about 135 pounds of meat from a 200-pound pig.

If you decide to start raising your own, start with a sow (female) and a boar (male). A sow can have two litters a year, with each litter producing five or six piglets. However, raising pigs can be difficult because pigs not only are prone to swine-based diseases, but they can also catch diseases that people carry. The more pigs you have, the higher their chances of catching something. If you are thinking about creating your own herd of pigs, be sure to talk to your local extension agent or veterinarian about the breeds that work best in your area, and the potential diseases.

 ### Self-Sufficient Facts, Knowledge, and Support
Truffles, highly prized subterranean mushrooms that can be sold for more than $800 per pound, are found with trained pigs. According to the Royal Philatelic Society London, French hunters of truffles have reported pigs can determine the presence of a truffle from 20 feet away.

In real estate, professionals often talk about "location, location, location." Those same words should be your utmost priority once you decide to raise pigs. When air fresheners talk about "Country Fresh" they are not referring to pig manure, which has a unique and penetrating odor. When you locate your site, you want to be sure that your home and your neighbors' homes are not downwind of the pigpen.

Once you decide where, you must create the right combination of shelter for your pig. First, it needs to be secure. Pigs are strong and can easily break through insufficient fences. They also root (dig in the soil with their noses) and can dig underneath a fence line and escape. So, you have to be sure that your fence line extends below the ground about 6" and is of high quality.

In warm weather, pigs need a place that is dry and provides shade; pigs have sweat glands on their snouts only and will sunburn and overheat quickly. This is why pigs enjoy rolling in the mud; the mud not only protects their skin, but it also helps to cool them down. If you can create a space in their pen for a dip in the mud, your pigs will be very happy. In cold weather, pigs need a dry place that is protected from the cold and wind.

Although pigs will eat large quantities of just about anything (that's where we get the term "eating like a pig"), they also need a balanced diet of grains (not just corn) in order to gain weight and have the correct meat-to-fat ratio. Pigs can be fed leftovers from your kitchen, the local vegetable processing plant, and even the local cheese processing plant. You just want to be sure that what you feed your pig is healthy and natural. Research what's available in your area and talk to your local extension agent for more information.

Raise Cattle

When you decide to raise a cow, you need to understand that you are looking at a long-term commitment. A cow can potentially live twenty years. During that lifespan, she can produce a calf every year and be milked for most of that time. The calves can be raised either for meat or to increase your herd.

The factors you need to consider before purchasing a cow are (1) space, (2) feed, and (3) your needs. A cow will need at least two acres of good pasture. During the time that she can't graze, you will need about 30 pounds of hay per day. If you need to feed your cow hay from the beginning of November to the beginning of April, you could easily need 2½ tons of hay. You will need a place to store the hay, as well as straw for bedding. Your cow will also need grain supplements throughout the year.

Depending on the breed you choose, an average cow can produce about six gallons of milk per day. After giving birth to a calf, a cow can produce milk for more than a year. However, a cow is generally rebred sixty to ninety days after the birth of her last calf and only milked for seven months while she is pregnant. The total gestation (the length of a pregnancy) time for a cow is 9½ months. A newborn calf will weigh about a hundred pounds, depending on the breed, and will be able to walk within an hour of being born.

Dairy cattle tend to be gentler animals than beef cattle and are better suited for a family farm. Within the dairy breeds, Jerseys, Guernseys, Brown Swiss, and Holsteins are the friendliest. Because of their smaller size and the high butterfat content of their milk, Jerseys can be the perfect cows for someone just starting out.

RAISE POULTRY

Chickens and other fowl are a great addition to any self-sufficient home, whether you have a farm sprawled across many acres or a humble plot with a small backyard. Relatively cheap and easier to care for than other livestock, poultry will produce meat and eggs for your family to enjoy year after year, and their personalities make them a joy to share your yard with.

Keep Chickens

If you are raising chickens for meat, you will find the most efficient feed-to-flesh conversion ratio with the Cornish Rock broiler. These hybrid chickens grow quickly and produce broad breasts and big thighs (think white meat and dark meat). But if you are buying chickens in order to create a flock that self-propagates, these are not the chickens for you. First, because they are hybrid, the chicks will not turn out like the parents. Second, because these chickens have been bred to grow so rapidly, they have been known to have heart attacks after three or four months.

There are slower-growing breeds that are both egg laying and meat producing; ask your local extension agent which slow-growing breeds are best for your area. These breeds are a wonderful choice for growing a small farm flock. The meat growth will take more time and you will have a lower feed-to-flesh conversion ratio, but you will not have the expense of buying new chicks year after year because you will be able to hatch your own. Generally in these situations, you take the roosters (males) and grow them for meat, because you only need one rooster (and perhaps a backup rooster) for your flock.

Self-Sufficient Facts, Knowledge, and Support
When you receive your day-old chicks, dip their beaks in water before you turn them loose. A baby bird will not instinctively go to the water and can die of dehydration standing right next to water.

Egg layers are often divided into Bantams and Standards. Bantams are very small birds and come in a variety of colors and types. They require less room and less feed than Standards, but they produce smaller eggs (three Bantam eggs equal two regular eggs in a recipe). Bantams are often raised as pets because they have great personalities, but don't let that fool you into thinking they aren't producers. Bantams make the best brooders (hens that sit on their eggs so they hatch), and soon you'll have a good-sized flock of Bantams.

Standards range from heavy breeds to light breeds. They include many of the breeds you might be familiar with: Wyandotte, Rhode Island Red, Plymouth Rock, and Barred Rock. Standards also include fairly unknown breeds such as Turkens (naked-necked chickens that look like turkeys), crested breeds, which have tufts of feathers around their heads, and feather-footed breeds. They can produce brown eggs or white eggs—some even produce colored eggs. No matter what color is on the outside of an egg, the inside is the same. However, if you are thinking about selling some of your excess eggs, brown eggs will bring you more money per dozen. (Brown eggs are priced higher because they come from larger chickens; hence, it costs more to feed these fowl, and their eggs are set at a higher price.) If you are raising a self-propagating flock, look for breeds that are good brooders.

Another resource you can use as you plan your first flock is the BackYard Chicken Forum (*www.backyardchickens.com*). This is a forum with many experienced chicken farmers who are willing to share their knowledge with beginners.

Think about Turkeys

Today's turkeys fall into two distinct categories: broad breasted and not broad breasted (or Heritage). The biggest of the breeds is the Broad Breasted White. These birds grow quickly and have remarkably meaty breasts. The tom turkeys (males) can actually end up dressing out (be ready for consumption) at 45 pounds, and hen turkeys (females) at 25 pounds. Their breast meat often extends above the breastbone, giving them a busty look. Their broad breasts limit their natural ability to reproduce and brood. But, unlike the Cornish Rock, their hearts won't give out after a few months. If you want to create a flock of this breed, you will need to artificially inseminate the hens and incubate the eggs.

When you picture the traditional Thanksgiving turkey, you are actually thinking of the Heritage Bronze Turkey, one of the not-broad-breasted turkey breeds. This breed is being left behind by the turkey industry because it does not grow as quickly as its broad-breasted counterpart. Yet these turkeys are better mothers and can be fertilized naturally. Their feed-to-flesh conversion ratio is not as high as the broad-breasted varieties, but they can still dress out at 10 to 25 pounds.

Turkey eggs are actually good to eat, but because the cost of purchasing turkey poults (newborn turkeys) is fairly high, the eggs should be incubated so you can grow your own flock.

CONSIDER THE COST OF VETERINARY VISITS

When your cat or dog gets sick or has other health issues, you probably take your pet to a veterinarian. Farmers don't do this with livestock unless their animals come down with something beyond their previous experience. It's not a matter of compassion; it's a matter of basic economics and professionalism. When you have a whole flock or herd of animals, hiring a vet for all their ailments moves beyond costly to prohibitively expensive. Moreover, as a farmer you need to be a professional at animal husbandry. That means it's your responsibility to learn everything you can about all the common ailments and diseases that the livestock you've chosen to raise are likely to suffer from and how to treat each of them yourself. Of course, when one of your animals is sick and you don't have a clue as to the cause, then you have little choice but to take the patient to a veterinarian. This will be a good time to cultivate a close relationship with the vet so you'll have someone to call when you're unsure of your own diagnoses.

Preserve Your Sustainable Lifestyle

Farm feed stores are your best source of affordable veterinary supplies. There you'll find antibiotics, reusable hypodermic needles, suitable restraints, and all the other items you'll need to keep your animals healthy and comfortable. It's a good idea to keep a little penicillin in your refrigerator at all times.

You'll want to know how to give vaccinations, how to assist difficult births, and, if such is necessary, how to do minor surgeries, such as dehorning, castration, and caponizing. This isn't for the faint of heart, but you can learn the techniques from an experienced farmer or a veterinarian. With a little practice you'll get to the point where you can do it without undue trauma to either the animal or yourself.

If you only have a few animals, that is, if they're more like pets than livestock, then you may not want to get this involved. However, if their numbers run into the dozens or more, then practicality will dictate that you learn these procedures from as knowledgeable a source as possible, be it a veterinarian or a veteran at animal husbandry. Of course, if you have only a handful of animals, then the simplest, cheapest solution would be to leave them intact and learn instead how to deal with their horns, testes, or other "undesirable" body parts. It's all just part of farming at your self-sufficient home.

CHAPTER 5

Pest Control

When you maintain a self-sufficient home, you will be exposed to "new neighbors." Depending on where your home is, these neighbors could be as innocuous as white-tailed deer and rabbits or as predatory as badgers and coyotes. Learning how to recognize and deal with these critters that will share your space is imperative. Dealing with pests can be handled violently or passively, depending on what works best; but there will never be a truce when managing them, because for every tomato you plant, every chick you hatch, or every morsel of food you raise and store, there's something else out there that wants the fruits of your labors every bit as much as you do.

IDENTIFY AND CONTROL RODENTS

One of the biggest problems you can encounter when you have your own home or farm is rodent infestation. The main issue with rats and mice is not the things they eat; it is the destruction they create when finding food. Rodents chew through items in your home or in your storage buildings. They will chew through plastic, wood, cardboard, and electrical wires. Rats have even been found to chew through lead pipes and concrete dams. When they find a food source, they will leave feces throughout the food they don't consume. This includes grain supplies for your livestock and even food supplies for your family.

There is never just one rodent. A pair of rats and their off-spring can produce 1,500 more rats within a twelve-month period. Because rodents are nocturnal, you need to look for the signs of infestation rather than assume that if you don't see them, they're not there. Look for the following signs to see if you have some unwelcome guests:

Self-Sufficient Facts, Knowledge, and Support
The feces and urine that rodents leave in food supplies are often very dangerous. *Salmonella* and *E. coli* cause gastrointestinal infections that have been linked to rodent infestation. Other diseases include hantavirus, a respiratory disease, as well as the plague and murine typhus.

Holes and Nests

The difference between rat holes and mice holes is size. A rat hole is about 3" in diameter. A mouse hole is one-quarter of that size, or about ¾". Rodent holes can be found outdoors under sheds, in outbuildings, around haystacks, and in refuse heaps. Inside, holes may be gnawed in floors, between walls, behind counters, and at baseboards. Both rats and mice make nests using whatever kind of material is available to them, including paper, cloth, grass, leaves, cardboard, and insulation material.

Smears

Rats like to move with their bodies in contact with a solid object, such as a wall. This contact will often create a greasy stain or smear on the wall. They also leave smears from their backs when they scramble under joists or other obstructions.

Runs

Rodents tend to travel using an established route. Outdoors you may be able to see the pathway or run in the vegetation around the outbuildings. Inside, unless the route travels through a dusty area, it is hard to locate.

Droppings

Droppings are a sure indicator that you have a rodent issue. The number of droppings, their position, and age will give you an idea of how many rodents you have and where they are moving and feeding. Fresh droppings are shiny, soft, and moist for a few hours. As they start to age they become duller and harder. Rat droppings are capsule-shaped and about ½" long; they are often found in groups on runs. Mice droppings are rod-shaped, less than ¼" long, and generally scattered.

Signs of Damage

The more rodents you have, the more extensive and obvious the damage. Damage can include holes gnawed through wood, plastic, cables, pipes, silage bags, and sacks. The holes made by rats will be larger than those made by mice.

SANITIZE AND RODENT-PROOF YOUR HOME

Successful rodent control involves three different facets: (1) sanitation, (2) rodent-proofing, and (3) rodent killing. Though the first two methods are most important, they also require the most effort and therefore are frequently neglected.

You must use tight lids on garbage cans, get rid of refuse, remove junk, and properly store food and construction materials. These steps will limit the food supply and nesting sites for rodents.

You should store food products in sealed cabinets or in glass or metal containers. Store feed for your livestock in metal containers, such as metal garbage cans, with tight-fitting lids. Be sure to clean up any spilled food. A well-swept floor makes it easier to detect signs of rodent activity.

Self-Sufficient Facts, Knowledge, and Support
Even though most people consider mice less disgusting than rats, mice are much more common and cause more damage. Mice are prolific breeders, producing offspring in great abundance. There are approximately five to ten babies per litter, with a new litter born every forty-five days or so. At eight weeks of age, the pups are capable of mating.

Rodent-proofing also involves looking at your home and your outbuildings to see how you can keep pests out. Inspect these areas thoroughly to find any trouble spots. Some areas you might consider are:

- All openings where water pipes, drain spouts, and vents enter a building. These should be tightly sealed with sheet-metal patches or, if they're not in use anymore, filled with concrete.
- Doors, windows, and screens should close tightly to ensure that rodents cannot enter through them. Check to see if window frames fit tightly against the foundation in the basement, especially in older homes.
- Install 24- to 26-gauge galvanized sheet-metal flashing around wooden door jambs and metal kick plates on the outside of doors to prevent rats from gnawing entrances under or around doors.
- Floor drains and fan openings should be tightly covered with galvanized hardware cloth, 19-gauge, ¼" mesh, so the rodents can't enter through them.
- Remove materials that are stacked against the outside of an otherwise rodent-proof building. This will stop rats and mice from gaining entry into upper stories.
- Nonconcrete basement floors, especially dirt floors, and shallow foundations should be protected from burrowing rats with a cement curtain wall around the outer edge extending 3 feet into the ground, or in an L-shape 2 feet into the ground, with a 1-foot lip extending outward.
- Check for any other possible entrances that are larger than ¼", and seal or block them so a rodent cannot get in.

If your rodent infestations are severe, you should work to kill the rodents first, before you remove their safe havens, to prevent them from just migrating to other nearby areas.

KILL UNWELCOME RODENTS

Trapping is the most common method of killing rodents. Traps may or may not be baited, but should always be placed in areas of rodent activity. Look for signs of droppings or runs and set up the traps there. Bacon, peanut butter, bread, and nutmeats are good baits for the traps.

Place mousetraps at intervals of about 3 to 4 feet. Rat traps should be set farther apart, about 15 to 30 feet. The most effective way to situate the trap is with the bait toward the wall and the spring away from the wall, because mice and rats tend to follow the wall line. Check the traps often, discard dead rodents, and reset the traps.

Rodenticide, or rat poison, is an alternative method of killing rodents. The rodent eats the poison and then goes back to the nest and dies. If you have rodents in your home, having the rodent die in the wall can create an unpleasant smell. Poison can be used effectively if you have rats in your outbuildings. However, do not use poison if you have small children or other animals on your property that might accidentally ingest the poison.

There are also traps on the market that consist of a sticky surface that attracts mice and rats. Once the rodent steps onto the surface, it is caught and cannot get away. Unlike a spring trap, which kills the rodent immediately by breaking its neck, these traps prolong death. Often you will come across live rodents stuck to the trap and screaming. To put them out of their misery, you can pick up the trap carefully and put it in a bucket of water so the rodent drowns.

PRACTICE INSECT CONTROL

If you have a garden, you will have an insect problem. Scientists estimate that there are 900,000 known species of insects, representing 10 quintillion individual bugs. Because there are so many insects that love fresh fruits and vegetables, it is wise to have a reference book, or website, with photographs or drawings so you can look up each new insect that comes to ruin your day and your garden. You'll find specific information about what to do to eliminate the little vandals, but for now you'll benefit from learning a few general techniques of insect control.

Prevention

As with other problems, the best solution is to take care of the problem before it happens. There are several things you can do to keep insects out of your crops in the first place:

- Use fertile, healthy soil: Studies have shown that strong, healthy plants are less likely to be attacked by insects than weak, marginal ones. Build up your soil with compost, mulch, and natural fertilizers.
- Get rid of weak plants: These not only are most susceptible to insect invasion, but they may invite it. Don't harbor plants that are clearly diseased or weak; they won't get any better, and they can endanger the rest of the garden.
- Rotate crops: It's not good to grow the same thing in the same place each year. Pests can overwinter in the soil, giving them a head start.
- Practice companion planting: The roots, leaves, and flowers of many herbs and vegetables attract beneficial insects or

repel harmful ones, usually by their scent. Learn all the best companions for the plants you grow, and then provide them with the company they prefer.

- Eliminate bug habitat: Clean up all the unnecessary weeds and debris that can harbor insect breeding grounds.
- Avoid standing moisture: Water the garden early in the day so that the moisture on the leaves will have time to dry out. Consider using soaker hoses or drip irrigation to keep your plants drier, which in turn will discourage insect and fungus growth.

Persistence is key when protecting your plants. As you water and care for your crops, make sure you're using the previous tips to safeguard from insects.

USE NATURAL INSECTICIDES

Whether you are looking for a natural insect deterrent for your garden or for yourself and your family, there are many options available that don't require you to spend a lot of money and won't have you worrying about exposure to harsh chemicals.

Diatomaceous Earth

Diatomaceous earth is actually made from tiny fossilized water plants. These water plants, called diatoms, were once algae-like plants but now are a sedimentary mineral. The sediment is mined and then ground up to a consistency that resembles talcum powder. However, if you were to look at diatomaceous earth through a microscope, you would see microscopic razor-sharp edges. These sharp, diamond-like particles either cut through an insect's outer layer or shred the insides of the insect if the dust is ingested.

Homemade Sprays

Many nontoxic ingredients found in your home are wonderful deterrents to insects. A simple spray consisting of liquid detergent and water will keep insects off nonedible houseplants and will also kill box-elder bugs. Bugs generally don't care for "hot" mixtures; one proven spray includes one crushed clove of garlic, one small chopped hot pepper, and one quart of water. This can be sprayed on plants to repel insects. There are many more recipes like this that include safe ingredients. Test them to see which ones work best for you.

Herbal Options

The plant world offers a wide array of options for repelling insects:

- Fly repellents: collect pennyroyal, rosemary, rue, southernwood, thyme, or tansy and hang them or stand them up in a vase where flies are bothersome. These plants were used during the Middle Ages to help repel flies.
- Ant and mite repellent: a strong decoction of walnut leaves (six handfuls of leaves boiled in one pint of water for twenty to thirty minutes) can be "painted" around floors or on work surfaces.
- Moth repellent: lay sprigs of dried herbs such as rosemary, southernwood, santolina, and lavender among blankets or woolens.
- Outdoor insect repellents: rub a handful of fresh elder leaves on your arms, legs, and neck. This works for about twenty minutes and then must be renewed. You can also use strong infusions of chamomile or elder leaves dabbed on the skin to prevent insect bites.

These natural repellants will protect your home, plants, and family safely, and without harsh chemicals.

Companion Planting

Many herbs can repel pests if you put them near the plants you wish to protect. Careful use of companion plants can protect your garden from pesky intruders. Here are some examples of companion plants:

Herb or Plant	Location	Benefit
Basil	plant near tomatoes	repels flying insects
Borage	plant near strawberries	improves crop yield, attracts bees
Caraway, buckwheat, flax	plant anywhere in the garden	improves the condition of the soil
Chamomile	plant anywhere in the garden, and near onions	repels flying insects, improves crop yield
Chives	plant near apple trees, roses	prevents scab, prevents black spot
Coriander	plant anywhere in the garden, and near anise	attracts bees, improves flavor
Dill, fennel	plant anywhere in the garden	attracts beneficial insects
French marigold	plant near tomatoes	repels aphids
Garlic	plant near roses	helps the overall health of the plant

Herb or Plant	Location	Benefit
Hyssop	plant near grapevines	improves crop yield
Mint	plant anywhere in the garden, and near cabbage	repels flies and cabbage grubs
Nasturtium	plant near apple trees, tomatoes, broad beans	repels aphids; attracts blackflies to itself, keeping the neighboring plants safe; repels ants; and keeps the garden healthy
Nettle	plant anywhere in the garden	controls blackflies
Pennyroyal	plant anywhere in the garden	repels ants
Rosemary	plant near carrots, sage	repels carrot fly; generally beneficial to sage
Sage	plant near cabbages, vines, rosemary, and anywhere for general garden use	repels cabbage moth; generally beneficial to the garden and repels a number of harmful flying insects
Summer savory	plant near beans	attracts bees and is generally beneficial

Be sure to care for your companion plants as you do for your regular crops; their well-being is directly connected to the health and production of your other plants.

GET RID OF BIRDS AND FLYING PESTS

Some people try to control birds in the garden with guns or poisons. These methods are neither safe nor effective. The very best way to control bird damage in your garden or orchard is with plastic bird netting, which is cheap and effective. Be sure that when you cover a plant or tree with netting, you tie it down at the base or stalk so that it doesn't blow away.

Additionally, you can try using scarecrows. These can be dummy humans, plastic snakes or owls, foil pie pans or old CDs hung on strings to catch the sunlight, or dark-colored cloths placed in the limbs of trees to simulate cats waiting for a bird to land.

Hawks, Eagles, and Owls

One of the few predators that hunt during the day, raptors—hawks and eagles—will capture a bird and tear the breast out of it. Hawks have even been known to attack through netting if they can push it down far enough to get to a chicken. In many states, raptors are protected by law. Check with your state department of natural resources or wildlife management before you try to capture this predator. If your chickens vanish at night without a trace, you have most likely been visited by an owl. Bringing your birds into a secure coop at night is the best deterrent against owls.

Flying Pests

In the recent past, the United States has been inundated with two new species of insects that have become overwhelming in both the home and the garden. One of these bugs, the Asian beetle, was actually brought to the United States by the government in the hope that it would be a solution for another problem. Unfortunately, the solution was worse than the initial problem. Wasps, on the other hand, have been around for a long time, but can be threatening to your family.

Asian Lady Beetles

The University of Kentucky College of Agriculture Extension Entomologists Michael F. Potter, Ric Bessin, and Lee Townsend's fact sheet "Asian Lady Beetle Infestation of Structures" stated:

> During the 1960s to 1990s, the U.S. Department of Agriculture attempted to establish the Asian lady beetle to control agricultural pests, especially of pecans and apples. Large numbers of the beetles were released in several states, including Georgia, South Carolina, Louisiana, Mississippi, California, Washington, Pennsylvania, Connecticut, and Maryland. . . .
>
> Large numbers of lady beetles (ladybugs) infesting homes and buildings in the United States were first reported in the early 1990s. Ladybugs normally are considered beneficial since they live outdoors and feed on plant pests.
>
> One species of lady beetle, *Harmonia axyridis*, can be a nuisance, however, when they fly to buildings in search

of overwintering sites and end up indoors. Once inside they crawl about on windows, walls, attics, etc., often emitting a noxious odor and yellowish staining fluid before dying.

Unfortunately, Asian lady beetles appear to lack natural enemies, although cold weather and freezing temperatures will kill some of them.

Asian lady beetles will start migrating into your home when autumn approaches. "Swarms of lady beetles typically fly to buildings from September through November, depending on locale and weather conditions," write Potter, et. al. These swarms "are heaviest on sunny days following a period of cooler weather, when temperatures return to at least the mid-60s. . . . They tend to congregate on the sunnier, southwest sides of buildings illuminated by afternoon sun. Homes or buildings shaded from afternoon sun are less likely to attract beetles. . . .

"Once the beetles alight on buildings, they seek out crevices and protected places to spend the winter. They often congregate in attics, wall cavities, and other protected locations. . . .

"Asian lady beetles generally do not injure humans and are mainly a nuisance. . . . Although Asian lady beetles do not transmit diseases *per se*, recent studies suggest that infestations can cause allergies in some individuals, ranging from eye irritation to asthma."

There are several things you can do to rid your home of Asian beetles:

- Caulk and seal entry points throughout your home.
- Place some glue traps on your windowsills. The Asian beetles will flock to the windows, get stuck on the traps, and die. You can simply replace the traps as they fill up.
- Vacuum up the beetles.

As with many other pests invading your home, persistence is essential in order to deal with swarms of lady beetles. But with these easy steps, you'll be able to keep their populations at bay.

Japanese Beetles

Just when you were getting used to Asian beetles, a new variety of beetle appeared on the scene in the United States: Japanese beetles. These bugs attack plants both as adults and as grubs (larvae). The adults eat the leaves and fruits of several hundred kinds of fruit trees, as well as ornamental trees, shrubs, vines, and crops, leaving behind large holes in the leaves.

As they develop, grubs attack the roots of trees and feed on the roots of various plants and grasses. Grubs have been known to destroy turf in lawns, parks, golf courses, and pastures.

Female adult beetles burrow about 3" into the ground and lay their eggs. One female can lay up to sixty eggs. The eggs hatch by midsummer, and the young grubs begin to feed, destroying the roots of the surrounding plants. When autumn is nearly over, the grubs will burrow into the soil and remain dormant until the following spring. In the spring, the grubs return to the turf and continue to feed until they change into pupae. Within two weeks, the pupae become adult beetles and emerge from the ground. Then the cycle begins again.

Although chemical insecticides are an option for killing both the beetle and the grub, you should consult with your county extension agent to determine what is allowed in your area. The most common way to eliminate Japanese beetles is to use commercial traps. Traps for adult beetles operate primarily with two chemical lures. A combination of a pheromone, or sex attractant, and a floral lure attract both male and female adult beetles to the trap. Then, as a result of their clumsy flying and the design of the trap, they end up caught in either the bag or funnel portion of the trap.

What you need to understand as you place your traps is that the pheromone in the trap will attract beetles from all around, so if you put the trap in the middle of your orchard, you are increasing your problem, not decreasing it. The best thing to do is find an area far away from your garden and orchard and hang the trap. Remember to check the trap, empty the bag, and then eliminate any beetles that are still alive.

Wasps

A wasp's stinger is not barbed like a honeybee's stinger, so a wasp can repeatedly sting its victim. If you are stung by a wasp, wash the area with soap and water, take an antihistamine, and apply ice to the sting. If you are stung by a wasp on more than one occasion, you can develop a dangerous allergic reaction to the sting. If you are allergic to bee stings and are stung by a wasp, seek medical care immediately. Also, if you are allergic to bees or wasps, ask your doctor about a prescription for the EpiPen, which you can carry with you.

To get rid of wasps, you first must locate the nest. Wasps not only build nests in elevated areas; they can also build nests underground. Your best clue is to watch for heavy wasp traffic during dusk or dawn, when wasps return to the nest. Wait for the sun to go down, as cooler temperatures impede the wasps' movement. Dress in protective clothing, including long sleeves and gloves, and spray the nest with an insecticide designed specifically for wasps. These insecticides generally have projectile shooting abilities, so you don't have to get too close to the nest. Spray liberally, but avoid inhaling too much of the poison. Most wasp poisons kill wasps on contact, but it's best to be safe by slowly leaving the area, as sudden movements can attract the wasps' attention.

Judiciously check the nest the next day to ensure that all of the insects have been killed. If not, repeat the process in the evening.

PROTECT AGAINST LARGER ANIMALS

One of the first things you should learn when establishing a self-sufficient home is what kinds of predators are common in the area. Your local extension agent will likely be an excellent source of information to get you started. The agent can give you an idea of what animals are prevalent in your area, can help you with any legal questions you may have about whether any of the predators are protected, and may also be able to help you find a reputable, knowledgeable trapper in your area. Here are a few of the predators that might be on your list:

Weasels

Weasels are found throughout the United States and are very destructive. Because weasels can enter a chicken coop through even a mouse-sized hole, they are almost impossible to keep out. As a preventive measure, you can nail hardware cloth over small holes to prevent them from getting into your chicken coop. A weasel will kill everything it can catch unless it is interrupted. You can tell that a weasel is the predator by a bite mark on the back of the prey's neck near the base of the skull. Weasels like to eat the entrails of poultry—the heart, liver, and kidneys.

However, your poultry is not the food of choice for weasels; they much prefer mice and rats. Weasels are very bold, curious animals and therefore are easy to trap. If you have pet mice, (gerbils, hamsters, etc.), you can save the cage cleanings and use those instead of bait. If you don't have cage cleanings, use fresh chicken liver as bait in a rat-sized snap trap. Set the traps near the holes and along the outside walls of outbuildings next to weeds that can provide cover.

Mink

The favorite hunting ground for mink is near water, although the males tend to travel longer distances than the females, especially during the winter breeding season. If you live in the country or anywhere near water, you need to be on guard against mink. Mink will kill poultry and small animals such as rabbits. You'll know if you've been visited by a mink because it will leave a distinctive musky smell. Mink eat large amounts of food and then den up for a period of time. If you don't catch it, a mink will be back in ten to fourteen days to kill again. Mink can be quite vicious, so if you suspect you have one attacking your livestock, contact a local trapper to catch this predator.

Skunks

You can generally tell when a skunk has been surprised; the unique skunk smell can permeate the air for miles. Skunks are generally not frequent predators, but if they can get into your coop, they will eat eggs and small chicks. The biggest problem is accidentally walking in on a skunk in your chicken coop. Skunks are easily caught in a cage trap baited with cat food. To calm the skunk before you move it, lay an old blanket slowly over the trap.

Opossums

Opossums are scavengers, and they often visit human homes or settlements to raid garbage cans, dumpsters, and other containers. They are attracted to carrion and can often be spotted near road-kill. Opossums will eat eggs, chicks, and adult birds. An opossum has razor-sharp teeth and uses its long rat-like tail as a fifth limb. When cornered, opossums will often "play dead," but they have also been known to be aggressive. They are easily caught in cage traps, and any food, even pet food, will work as bait. Opossums also carry a disease that is spread through their feces that can be fatal to horses, so extra care should be taken in and around stables.

Foxes

The best clue that a fox has raided your henhouse is that there will be little evidence other than a missing bird. You may find a few feathers or a wing, but a fox will usually take the bird with it unless it has been disturbed during the kill. A good dog or lights around the building will likely deter foxes, as foxes are normally quite shy. The term "clever as a fox" was coined for good reason. If you suspect a fox to be your predator, you should call an experienced trapper to help you catch it.

Self-Sufficient Facts, Knowledge, and Support
Foxes are omnivores. They are solitary hunters and eat rodents, insects, worms, fruit, birds, eggs, and all kinds of small animals. About 60 percent of a red fox's diet is made up of rabbits and mice. Foxes are very fast animals and usually catch their prey by out-running them.

Raccoons

Raccoons are strong and intelligent animals with paws that are very dexterous. Raccoons are able to tear through poultry netting and will even pull a bird right through larger, heavier fencing if they can grab any part of the bird. Finding a head that was bitten off a bird is a sure sign that your predator is a raccoon. A female with kits can destroy large numbers of birds in a short period of time. There are several raccoon-specific traps that are safe to use around dogs and cats. Raccoons are not afraid of traps and are easily caught using fish baits, such as wet or dry cat food.

Coyotes

Coyotes return often to good hunting grounds. If one of these predators has raided your farm, you can bet it will be back for more. The best signs that coyotes are around are the howls you hear in the evening. A large dog can deter a coyote, but coyotes often travel in packs and know how to work together to overpower a dog. The best means to rid yourself of this kind of predator is calling an experienced trapper, securing your livestock, and adding an electric fence.

Big Predators

In some areas of the country it is not unusual to lose livestock to mountain lions, bears, and wolves. These predators can kill larger livestock and endanger you and your family. If you suspect that a large predator is hunting on your property, contact your local department of natural resources or wildlife management to learn about your options for removing the animal.

WATCH OUT FOR CANINE DISTEMPER

On occasion, you might come across an animal "acting strangely" on your property; for example, a nocturnal animal may be out during the day, or an animal that is generally timid might wander into your dog run. When animals display characteristics that are unnatural, you need to suspect rabies or canine distemper.

Canine distemper is actually caused by a virus. The virus is related to rubella (the measles virus), but canine distemper poses no threat to humans. However, your domestic animals are at risk because the disease is highly contagious. Distemper affects a large variety of carnivores in North America. These animals include raccoons, foxes, skunks, weasels, and coyotes.

The majority of distemper cases are seen in the spring and summer because young animals are the most susceptible to the disease, but distemper can appear year-round. Cases of distemper can appear as widespread outbreaks or as just isolated cases.

Although the virus does not survive for very long outside the host body, a healthy animal can catch canine distemper either from direct contact with an infected animal or from its bodily secretions and waste. And because many of the symptoms an animal exhibits when it has distemper mimic the symptoms of rabies, you need to contact a physician immediately if you are bitten by an animal exhibiting any unusual behavior. The only way to be sure the animal has distemper rather than rabies is to test the brain tissue.

The symptoms of distemper are the same in all susceptible animals. The signs you should look for are obvious distress, coughing, sneezing, loose bowels, discharge from eyes and/or nostrils, and eyelids that are crusted over and stuck together. Infected animals can also have convulsions, tremors, and chewing fits. Because of their distress, these animals may lose their fear of humans. You should be very wary because they can become aggressive when approached. The animal may also exhibit dizziness and awkward movements.

If you suspect that an animal has distemper, you must be sure to keep your pets and children away. If you need to destroy the animal or if it dies in your yard, be sure to either bury it deep enough to discourage your pet from digging it up or place it in a secure container and dispose of it in the trash. Wear gloves when disposing of the animal. Do not try to catch a diseased animal. If the animal is threatening you, your children, or your pets, you should kill it. To keep you and your family safe, make sure your pets are vaccinated against distemper.

CHAPTER 6
The Self-Sufficient Pantry

When you are living in a self-sufficient home, you may not have the ability to just run out to the corner supermarket. Indeed, one of the benefits of being self-sufficient means you don't *have* to visit the supermarket each week because you have most or all that you need on hand already. As such, you need a well-stocked pantry that not only creates a foundation for the things you like to eat, but also provides a resource for you and your family during harsh weather and lean times. Read on to discover how to stock and maintain an efficient, reliable pantry.

BUY BASIC COOKING SUPPLIES

Many of the foods you might have purchased at the local supermarket before you began a self-sufficient home will now be homemade—more delicious and definitely better for you. To ensure that your cooking efforts aren't frustrated, be sure you have a pantry that is stocked with the essentials you need. You can go to a warehouse store and buy many of these items in bulk. There are also wonderful cookbooks available that show you how to make some of your favorite items at home. The following list suggests supplies you should keep on hand; be sure to create your own list to include the things your family likes.

- Baking powder, baking soda, and yeast
- Bouillon cubes (beef and chicken)
- Condiments
- Cornstarch
- Cream of tartar
- Dry buttermilk
- Dry milk
- Dutch cocoa
- Nuts
- Oil
- Parchment paper, aluminum foil, plastic wrap, and plastic storage bags
- Raisins, dates, and other dried fruits
- Salt—iodized, pickling, kosher, and sea salt
- Shortening
- Soy sauce
- Spices and extracts
- Sugar, brown sugar, confectioner's sugar, honey, and molasses
- Vinegar
- Worcestershire sauce

Other helpful items you might want to have on hand are muffin and pancake mixes, gravy and seasoning mixes, various types of pasta, rice, potato flakes, and peanut butter and jelly.

Preserve Your Sustainable Lifestyle

Just because you are self-sufficient does not mean you must deprive yourself of your favorite comfort foods. Whether you want something that reminds you of happy childhood times or you simply want to indulge, comfort food is important. Family favorites can really help as you make the transition to living the self-sustaining lifestyle. Make a list of the foods your family loves and can't do without, and make sure you keep some in your pantry.

HAVE THE RIGHT EQUIPMENT ON HAND

The most important items a tradesman has are the tools of his trade. You wouldn't want to be a carpenter, plumber, or electrician without the proper specialized equipment that makes the job run smoother and helps you to be more efficient. The same could be said about the tools in a kitchen, especially a kitchen that is going to be an essential part of your daily life.

Because you are self-sufficient, you'll want to take your energy sources into account—whether traditional energy sources or the energy you are going to be able to produce yourself—as you look at appliances for your kitchen. That being said, even though some appliances might pull a great deal of electricity for a short amount of time, the savings in labor might be well worth it. Keep in mind, too, that your basic kitchen appliances—refrigerator, chest freezer, oven, stovetop, and dishwasher—should be Energy Star rated.

The next level of kitchen appliances—mixer, grinder, and food processor—should be of the best quality you can afford because you will use them often. However, cost does not always equate to quality, so be sure to read reviews of the items you want to purchase. A stand mixer with a dough hook and other attachments is an item you will use every day. If you can find one that has attachments for other kitchen tasks, such as grinding, slicing, or juicing, so much the better.

Preserve Your Sustainable Lifestyle

Think twice before buying a highly specialized appliance such as a bread machine. Often you will be baking more bread than the machine can handle, and you will be wasting both money and space for a machine that can only do one thing.

Canning supplies are essential. You can purchase them new or find them at garage sales, estate auctions, and online auctions. When buying used supplies, look for items such as steam juicers, cherry pitters, food strainers, and large water-bath canners. The items you will want to purchase new are pressure cookers and your canning tool set. You can buy new jars or pick them up at auctions or garage sales; just be sure they aren't chipped. You will need to buy new rings and lids.

Buy good-quality cookware, and be sure you also have cast-iron cookware. Cast iron is solid and dependable and can take a lot of abuse. The iron also leaches into the food you cook, increasing your iron intake.

You should have a good-quality hand-operated can opener. If you now use an electric model, you can continue to use it. But, in the event of a power outage, you will want to have a nonelectric opener close by.

Buy quality kitchen hand tools that will last and won't melt when exposed to hot surfaces. Imagine doing your everyday cooking and baking without electricity, and then buy the tools that would make that job easier.

Have at least one good set of measuring cups and spoons and several larger Pyrex multicup measuring cups. Purchase good-quality mixing bowls and bakeware. Be sure you have enough so you can bake several loaves of bread or sheets of cookies at the same time.

STOCK UP ON GRAINS

Grains are both an essential part of a healthy diet and a basic staple as an emergency food. Humankind has been harvesting grain for thousands of years. Archaeological digs have found evidence of the use of grains as far back as 9000 B.C.E. For many cultures, grains are a dietary staple. For your own self-sufficient home, grains act as food staples in your pantry and are used for creating flour, breads, sprouted grains, and oatmeal. They also serve as a delicious backdrop for many dishes to serve your family. Plus, they'll keep for months at a time should you face an emergency and need to rely on your own supplies.

Wheat

If you are looking for one source that could be a survival food, it would be wheat. Wheat is not only a nutty-tasting grain that makes wonderful bread and muffins, but you can also use wheat as a meat substitute, a vegetable, and a source of vitamin C and antioxidants. That is why wheat should be part of your family's long-term food storage plan.

You can store whole-kernel grain for a long time in a dry, cool area, but once you grind it, you should store it in your refrigerator because the oil in the kernel can spoil and the flour can turn rancid. Wheat is classified in three ways: the season of growth (winter or spring), whether it has a soft or hard kernel, and whether the bran layer is colored red or white. Generally, hard wheat is higher in protein and can be stored longer than soft wheat, although soft wheat is the wheat of choice for pastry flour.

Self-Sufficient Facts, Knowledge, and Support

Bulgur is white or red, hard or soft whole-wheat kernels that have been boiled, dried, slightly scoured, cracked, and sifted for sizing. The result is par-cooked cracked wheat. Bulgur may be sold as a pilaf or tabouli mix and may be called tabouli wheat. In stores, bulgur can be found near the pasta, rice, or hot cereal, or in a specialty food aisle.

When you purchase wheat, you should buy it from a reputable mill. The protein count should be no less than 12 to 14 percent and the moisture count should be under 10 percent. Make sure you store your wheat in a cool location in tightly sealed containers.

Wheat can be used in a variety of ways:

- Cooked unground wheat
- Flour
- Gluten
- Sprouts
- Wheat grass

Cooked Unground Wheat

To get the goodness from the whole grain, you can add boiling water and whole-kernel wheat to a thermos and let it sit overnight. In the morning, the wheat will have swelled to double in bulk and softened. You can eat it like a hot breakfast cereal with honey, dried fruit, and milk. You can also use wheat as a meat substitute in a casserole. Just make sure you add additional water and allow the casserole to bake until the wheat is tender.

Self-Sufficient Facts, Knowledge, and Support

All-purpose flour is white flour milled from hard wheat or a blend of hard and soft wheats. It gives the best results for many kinds of products, including some yeast breads, quick breads, cakes, cookies, pastries, and noodles. All-purpose flour is usually enriched and may be bleached or unbleached. Bleaching will not affect nutrient value. Different brands will vary in performance. Protein varies from 8 to 11 percent.

Flour

When you are going to use wheat for flour, you need a grain mill. An electric mill makes the job easier; however, it is wise to also purchase a hand mill in case of emergencies. Whole-wheat flour has more nutrients, protein, and fiber than bleached white flour. It can be substituted for part or all of the all-purpose flour in most recipes. You should experiment with your favorite recipes by substituting more whole-wheat flour for all-purpose each time. Because whole-wheat flour is denser, if you are going to replace the all-purpose flour completely, use ⅞ cup whole-wheat in place of 1 cup white. If you grind the wheat coarsely, you have cracked wheat. Cracked wheat can be used as a hot cereal and can be added to bread recipes to give the bread a nuttier taste.

Gluten

Gluten is the protein substance left when the starch has been taken out of the wheat. Gluten is often used as a meat substitute and can be flavored to taste like meat, fish, or poultry. Gluten is made by grinding the wheat, adding water to form a dough, and kneading and rinsing the dough to wash away the starch. Gluten is rich in protein just like beef, but it doesn't have any of the animal fat and the cholesterol. It is a great meat substitute, especially in casseroles.

Sprouts

Wheat can also be sprouted. This turns wheat from a simple grain into a vitamin-packed vegetable. HealthRecipes.com (*http:// healthrecipes.com/growing_sprouts.htm*) describes it this way:

> As water is introduced, enzyme inhibitors are disabled and the seed explodes to life. Germination unfolds, and enzymes trigger elaborate biochemical changes. Proteins break into amino acids. Water-soluble vitamins such as B complex and vitamin C are created. Fats and carbohydrates are converted into simple sugars. . . . Through the miracle of germination, thiamin increases five-fold and niacin content doubles. Vitamin C, E, and carotene increase. In fact, the vitamin C content becomes as rich as tomatoes.

Wheat Grass

When you "sow" wheat, just like you would any seed, the plant that grows looks like regular grass you would find on any lawn in the Midwest. But wheatgrass is not just any grass. You can grind wheatgrass to make a juice that contains chlorophyll, ninety minerals, and vitamins A, B complex, C, E, and K. Wheatgrass is extremely rich in protein and contains seventeen amino acids, the building blocks of protein. Wheatgrass helps to build your immune system and maintain a good metabolism. Although the most popular way to use wheatgrass is to turn it into juice, it can also be used in salads.

Oats

Although most people often think of oats or oatmeal as a breakfast food, it is much more versatile than just porridge. Oats make an excellent thickener of soups and stews and good fillers in meat loafs and casseroles. Cookies, granola, and granola bars are the next most typical ways to use oatmeal. All oats are processed to at least some extent before you can use them. The most common way to purchase them is as rolled oats, which have been cut and rolled using special equipment. However, you also can purchase oat groats, which are the whole oat with the hulls removed, and steel cut oats, which are groats that have been cut into smaller pieces with steel blades. Both take longer to cook than traditional rolled oats, but they add fiber and nutrients.

Rice

Rice is a staple in the diet for much of the world's population. It produces more food energy per acre than other cereal grains, and is second only to wheat in importance as a food cereal and in terms of protein per acre produced. Rice is classified in two ways: the way the grain is processed and the length of the grain. The processing methods affect the nutritional value of the rice:

■ Brown rice is the whole grain with only the hull removed. Brown rice keeps all of the nutrition of the grain and has a nutty flavor. It's the best choice as far as nutrition is concerned. However, the oil in the rice germ can become rancid, so brown rice only has a shelf life of about six months. There are distributors who can provide special packaging that seals the rice for long-term storage. However, once opened, the rice needs to be used within six months.

■ Converted rice is soaked, steamed, and partially cooked before it is dried, hulled, and polished to remove the bran and the germ. It is more nutritious than polished white rice, and its storage life is the same as regular white rice.

■ White rice has had its outer layers milled off. This process removes about 10 percent of the protein and most of the fat and mineral content. That's why white rice sold in the United States has to be "enriched" with vitamins to partially replace what was lost through processing. White rice has a long shelf life, up to five years, if stored in a cool, dry place.

■ Instant rice is fully cooked and then dehydrated, so all you need to do is reconstitute it. Instant rice has fewer calories and carbohydrates and less protein than regular rice.

Rice grain length is classified in these three ways:

1. Short grain rice is softer and moister when it cooks and tends to stick together. It is a little sweeter and has a stronger flavor than long grain rice.

2. Medium grain rice has a flavor similar to the short grain, but with a texture closer to long grain.

3. Long grain rice cooks up drier and flakier than the shorter types. The flavor is blander than short grain. It is the most common rice found in grocery stores.

Self-Sufficient Facts, Knowledge, and Support
In Japan and Indonesia, rice has its own god. The Chinese devote a whole day of their New Year celebration to the crop. In some Asian cultures, rice is considered a link between heaven and earth. The people of India believe rice is important to fertility, which explains the long-standing tradition of throwing rice at a wedding.

Corn

Corn is the largest grain crop in the United States, but the majority is used for animal feed or sold to food processors to make corn sweeteners. Corn can be purchased as kernels or ground (cornmeal), but the kernels will last longer in storage. Popcorn can either be used for snacking or it can be ground into a meal, but you should check with your mill manufacturer to be sure that your mill will grind popcorn.

Barley

Barley can be purchased in two forms: pearl barley, which has had the hull removed and has been polished, and pot or hulled barley, which has been processed, but not as much as pearl barley. The hulled barley retains more of the nutritious germ and bran. As with wheat, the oils in the germ can spoil over time, so hulled barley does not keep as well or as long as pearl barley. Whole barley is commonly used to add thickness to soups and stews.

Millet

Millet is less known in the United States but is a staple grain in North China and India. The grain kernels are small, round, and usually ivory-colored or yellow. When cooked like rice, millet makes an excellent breakfast cereal. Millet mixes well with other flours and adds a pleasant crunch when you add it to your homemade breads.

Sorghum

Although sorghum might be more familiar in the United States as a cousin to molasses, it is actually a principal cereal grain in South Africa. The small, round brown seeds can be cooked and used like rice or as a hot cereal. Although sorghum is low in gluten, the seeds can be milled into flour and mixed with higher-gluten flours for use in baking, or used alone for flat breads, pancakes, or cookies.

Rye

Rye has dark brown kernels that are longer and thinner than wheat kernels, but it also has less gluten and less protein. The flavor of rye flour is richer than wheat, and although you might associate rye with pumpernickel or black bread, it can be found in versions ranging from dark whole-grain flour to a lighter, more processed flour.

LEAVE ROOM FOR LEGUMES

Few nonanimal foods contain the amount of protein found in legumes. However, the protein found in legumes is not a complete protein and needs to be combined with the proteins found in grains. This is why you will find that throughout many cultures, legumes and grains (such as beans and rice) are traditionally served together. Legumes include beans, peas, lentils, and peanuts. Legumes can also be ground and the flour can be added to breads and soups to increase the protein. Legumes generally have a long shelf life if kept in an area that is cool and dry. Like grains, when properly stored, legumes can provide a source of nutrition for you and your family over a long period of time, especially when all other food sources become scarce. If you truly desire to stay self-sufficient, keep legumes on hand at all times, and you'll ensure a healthy food supply for your loved ones.

Self-Sufficient Facts, Knowledge, and Support
Because legumes contain small amounts of certain uric acid–forming substances (chemically known as *purins*), they should be avoided by people with gout. However, soybeans, chickpeas (garbanzo beans), etc., contain flavonoids, which work as the female hormone estrogen, providing women some relief from menopausal symptoms such as hot flashes.

Adzuki Beans

These small, deep-red beans are popular in Asia. You might have tasted them if you have ever had sweet bean paste in Chinese buns and other dishes. To cook, it's best to presoak them and then boil. Their flavor is milder than kidney beans, but they can be used in chili or other dishes that traditionally use kidney beans.

Black Beans

Black beans are common in Central and South American cuisine. They are small, dark brownish-black, and oval shaped. Because of their tendency to "bleed" once cooked, the beans should be rinsed before they're added to other recipes to avoid a "muddy" appearance in the dish.

Black-Eyed Peas

Popular in the southern part of the United States, black-eyed peas are also known as cowpeas or field peas. They are small and cream colored with a distinctive black spot on them. They cook quickly, and traditionally are combined with rice or cornbread.

Chickpeas

The primary ingredient in hummus and falafel, chickpeas (also known as garbanzo beans) are one of the oldest cultivated legumes. They are tan or cream colored and larger than most beans. Their unusual round kernel shape and nutty flavor make them a favorite ingredient in salads. They retain their firmness even after cooking and are often used in Indian cooking.

Great Northern Beans

These white, mild-tasting beans take on the flavor of the other ingredients with which they're prepared. Often used in soups, salads, and baked beans, the Great Northern is versatile and one of the most commonly eaten beans in the United States.

Kidney Beans

Although most people think of kidney beans as reddish-brown, they also can be white, mottled, or light red. One thing won't change—the familiar kidney bean shape. Kidney beans are meaty and have a distinct taste. Kidney beans are used in three-bean salad, chili, and many soups.

Lentils

Lentils are not a bean and not a pea—they have their own distinct classification in the legume family. They are high in protein and fiber and can be a substitute for meat. They are also high in folate and potassium. Unlike other legumes, lentils cook quickly without presoaking. Be sure to rinse them well before adding them to recipes. You can also just boil them until tender and add seasonings of your choice. They are delicious over rice or mixed with vegetables.

Lentils come in three main varieties: brown, green, and red.

- Brown lentils are the least expensive and are best used for soups because they soften when they are cooked and can get mushy.
- Green lentils are also known as French lentils. They have a nuttier taste. They are a good choice for salads because they stay firm after they've been cooked.
- Red lentils are the fastest-cooking lentil. Although they start out red, when cooked they quickly lose their shape and turn golden yellow. Their taste is sweeter and milder than their counterparts, and they are often used in Indian cooking.

Lima Beans

Also known as "butter beans," lima beans are another common legume. Their shape is flat and broad and rounded. They have a slightly sweet flavor that is a little bland, and are one of the main ingredients in succotash. Their color can range from pale green to speckled cream and purple.

Mung Beans

Mung beans are best known for their sprouts, but they are also common in Indian and Asian dishes. They are related to the field pea, with a similar shape but a darker color, ranging from medium-green to nearly black.

Navy Beans

Navy beans are similar to Great Northern beans, but they are smaller and retain their shape well when they are cooked. They are often used commercially for pork and beans. They received their name because they were a staple food of the United States Navy in the early twentieth century.

Peanuts

Peanuts are not traditional nuts like walnuts, pecans, etc. They actually grow underground, like potatoes, and are considered a legume. Peanuts have high protein and a good deal of fat. Peanuts can be ground for peanut butter, roasted, or baked, and in some regions of the United States, they are boiled.

Peas

Yellow or green, dried peas are often used in soups and also in Indian cuisine. If the peas are whole, they will need to be soaked before you cook them; however, dried split peas can be used without soaking. Split peas are best known for their use in split-pea soup.

Pinto Beans

Pinto beans are the most widely consumed legume in the southwestern area of the United States. Small, oval, and reddish-tan, pinto beans are used for refried beans, soups, and many Tex-Mex dishes.

If there were a national emergency and daily life as you know it was suspended, if trucks could no longer deliver goods, if the grid went down, if martial law were imposed and you and your family were basically on your own, what are the things you would need to survive?

Of course, you don't need a national emergency or a disaster to have to live in survival mode. What would happen if you lost your job and weren't able to get employment for months or years? What would happen if you were sick for an extended period of time? How would you care for your family?

You can learn about basic foods and concepts in order to be prepared for these eventualities. In this small section, you will learn about the basics you need to have in your pantry. However, there are many other excellent ideas about preparedness that should be incorporated into your self-sufficient lifestyle. Two excellent books that go into great detail about this kind of preparedness are *The New Passport to Survival* by Rita Bingham and *Making the Best of Basics* by James Talmage Stevens.

According to Rita Bingham, there are seven survival foods—grains, legumes, sprouting seeds, honey, salt, oil, and powdered milk. Grains and legumes have already been covered in this chapter, and you've also learned a little about sprouts, but there is still more to learn.

Sprouts

Unless you can bottle or freeze them, it's hard to store leafy green vegetables for a long period of time. You have probably pulled a bag of lettuce out of your refrigerator only to find that it has gone bad between the time you purchased it and the time you wanted to use it. But those green vegetables are essential to your health. So, how can you offer your family a supplement of high-powered greens? Sprouts.

From their original state as seeds, beans, or grains, sprouts actually increase in vitamins A, B, C, E, and K as they grow. Riboflavin and folic acid increase up to thirteen times, and vitamin C increases up to 600 percent.

You will want to offer your family a variety of sprouts in order to ensure a balanced diet. Many of the legumes and grains discussed in this chapter are excellent choices for sprouting, including wheat, barley, chickpeas, mung beans, adzuki beans, peas, and lentils. Other good choices for sprouts are alfalfa, buckwheat, clover, and quinoa. It's suggested that a one-month supply of beans for one adult would be about five pounds.

Nonfat Dry Milk

Nonfat dry milk, or powdered milk, is an excellent source of protein, calcium, and nutrition. It provides about 80 calories per serving. Most vitamins in dried milks are present in levels comparable to those of whole milk. However, vitamins A and D are not present in nonfat milk and must be supplemented.

Nonfat powdered milk can be used not only in cooking and baking, but also to create other dairy products, such as yogurt, cheese, and sour cream. Dried whole milk and dried buttermilk contain milk fat and are not suitable for long-term storage.

If you have milk allergies, consider other options. If your family enjoys soy milk, you can actually learn how to make your own with stored soybeans.

A month's supply of dry milk for one adult would be about 1½ pounds.

Honey

For more than 10,000 years, honey has been considered a basic survival food, both for its food qualities and for its medicinal purposes. Honey is a natural and healthy sweetener. It will store almost indefinitely, and comes in a variety of flavors depending on what plants the bees were exposed to as they gathered nectar and pollen.

Because honey isn't processed like sugar, it retains its nutrients and mineral content. And, because it is a natural food, it is digested more easily than sugar.

Honey also provides natural antioxidants that can boost your immune system. In addition, honey produced locally may help inhibit allergies.

Self-Sufficient Facts, Knowledge, and Support
Ancient Greeks and Romans referred to honey as a food fit for the gods. Greek custom was to offer honey to the gods and deceased spirits. This tribute kept one out of harm's way and in a spirit's or god's good graces.

Honey can be substituted in recipes calling for sugar. Simply use ¾ cup honey for every cup of sugar in the recipe. Because honey is liquid, as opposed to sugar, you should reduce the amount of liquid called for in the recipe by one-quarter. Honey will also give your foods a sweeter taste than sugar.

Honey can be stored in any clean container, from plastic food-grade buckets to glass jars. Honey should be stored at about 75°F, but if it is stored at a cooler temperature, the crystallization that occurs can be reversed by placing the container in warm water.

You should be aware that honey is not recommended for infants under the age of twelve months, as it can cause infant botulism.

You should store about 5 pounds of honey or sugar per adult per month.

Salt

Salt improves the flavor of foods. It is essential in many recipes for baked goods (it helps bread rise) and in canning and preserving food. The recommended amount of salt to store for a year's use is 8 pounds per person. Salt can be stored long-term and, if it cakes up, can be dried at a low temperature (250°F) in an oven until you can break it up so it is granulized again. Eating iodized salt is recommended to prevent goiter.

Oil

Fats are essential to your survival and for the structure and healthy functioning of your body. The body needs two essential fatty acids: linoleic acid, which is better known as omega-6 fatty acid, and linolenic acid, also known as alpha-linolenic, ALA, a type of omega-3 fatty acid. For general health, you should have a balance between omega-6 and omega-3 fatty acids. The ratio should be in the range of 2:1–4:1, omega-6 to omega-3.

Omega-3 fatty acid can be found in deep-water fish, fish oil, canola oil, flaxseed oil, and walnut oil. You can also find it in almonds, hazelnuts, pecans, cashews, walnuts, and macadamia nuts. Omega-6 fatty acids are found in raw nuts, seeds, legumes, and vegetable oils such as borage oil, grape seed oil, evening primrose oil, sesame oil, and soybean oil. When you store oil, be sure that you choose an oil that will help you meet your requirements of fatty acids.

It is suggested that for one month's storage you have about 1 quart of oil per adult.

CHAPTER 7

Canning and Preserving

If you have grown your own fruits and vegetables as a part of your self-sufficient lifestyle, you will find that there is nothing as satisfying as looking at row after row of jars on the shelves in your kitchen that contain the literal fruits of your labors. You've planted, watered, and weeded, and tended your animals, and now you're starting to reap the benefits. You've got fresh food by the bucketful, but the job isn't over yet. Now it's time to put away the bounty you've created over these last few months and enjoy a pantry full of the best foods you've ever had.

Canning and preserving was the way our ancestors stored foods for the winter months—but as you continue to practice sustainable living, you'll find that you can enjoy your preserved goods year-round. The best part of preserving your bounty (besides saving money on groceries, shopping trips, and throwing away spoiled food) is knowing that your family will be well fed with nutritious and incredibly delicious food.

LEARN TO PRESERVE YOUR OWN FOODS

Canning is a bit labor intensive, but it has some outstanding advantages. For example, once food has been canned, it has a long shelf life and can be kept about any place in the home. With canning, you can preserve foods until your home is bursting at the seams with stored food. You also don't need to make a large investment such as buying a deep freezer; all that's required for canning is a canning kettle or a pressure cooker and as many canning jars as you need to do the job.

Choosing a Proper Canning Method

How you will can your food depends on its pH content. The more acidic the food, the less heating time or less heat is required to destroy bacteria. Foods with less acidity need more time or more heat in order to make them safe. Most fruits are more acidic and can be canned using a water-bath method. However, vegetables such as corn and beans are less acidic and so must be canned using a pressure cooker. Tomatoes have always been in the middle, and water-bath canning was considered fine. Recently, however, researchers discovered that the acid content of tomatoes depends on where they were grown as well as their variety and ripeness.

Food Safety

It is imperative that you can your foods for the correct amount of time and in the correct manner. You must sterilize the food and the container with high heat and then pack the one inside the other. High-acid foods (pickles, tomatoes, fruits, etc.) need to be sterilized at boiling temperature (212°F, 100°C), but low-acid foods such as meat, dairy products, and vegetables can develop dangerous toxins if not processed at 240°F (116°C) or higher, which makes the pressure cooker necessary for these foods.

Sealing the jars creates a vacuum that protects the color, flavor, and nutritional elements of the food inside and protects against rancidity from oxidation. When canning, if you live at a higher elevation (over 1,000 feet, or 305 meters, above sea level) you'll need to increase the water-bath processing time. This compensates for the lower temperature of boiling water at high altitudes, because the atmospheric pressure is lower the higher you go.

Botulism toxin is one of the most deadly poisons known on earth. If you merely touch a finger to it and touch that finger to your lips to taste, you could get enough toxins to kill you. Luckily, botulism cases are rare, but one death is too many. This isn't meant to frighten you away from home canning, because hundreds of thousands of people successfully home can their produce every year. This is to remind you that you cannot take shortcuts when it comes to preserving your food.

Preserve Your Sustainable Lifestyle

The National Center for Home Food Preservation's website *http://nchfp.uga.edu* is a rich source of information on all types of food preservation, but especially canning. There you can find detailed instructions on how to can just about any specific foods you might want to preserve.

Essential Equipment

Before you begin canning, look at your equipment, especially your jars. Most canning jars are made to be used year after year. Throw away any chipped or cracked jars. Canning lids are meant to be used only once. Throw away any old canning lids. Rings can be used over and over again, unless they don't fit tightly. Have the canning equipment clean and ready to use so as to get the canning done quickly when the produce is at its freshest state possible.

CHOOSE A CANNING METHOD

Once your harvest is ready to be canned, you have some options when it comes to the method by which you preserve it. The two most common methods are water-bath canning (also known as steam-bath canning) and pressure-cooker canning. As stated earlier, the acidity of the food you plan to can determines the method you must use. Be sure to refer to "Choosing a Proper Canning Method" to determine which method is best for your crop.

Water-Bath Canning

For water-bath or steam-bath canning you need jars, lids, rings, a canning kettle, a rack, and a jar lifter. Place the prepared fruit in sterile, clean hot jars, covered with either water or syrup, depending on your recipe. Put the lid and ring on immediately and tighten. Lower the jar into your kettle of boiling water. You will need a rack on the bottom of your kettle for the jars to sit on. Without a rack, the jars could break. The kettle has to be tall enough and the water deep enough so the water will cover the jars by at least 1" to 2" at all times. If the processing will take a long time, have an auxiliary kettle filled with boiling water waiting to replace the evaporated water. Once you have filled the kettle with your jars, make sure the water is at a boil, place the lid on the kettle, and set your timer.

When the correct amount of time has passed, remove the jars with a jar lifter and place them on top of a towel or wooden board on your table or counter. As they cool you will hear the sound of pop-ping, which indicates the lids have sealed.

Start timing your next batch once the water has come to a boil again.

Self-Sufficient Facts, Knowledge, and Support
Botulism is caused by a certain kind of bacterium, *Clostridium botulinum*, that is practically everywhere in the soil. The bacteria themselves are not poison-ous in their dormant state. However, when heated, the spores in the bacteria begin to grow and form a toxin. The spores are resistant to heat and thrive in an airless, low-acid, and low-sugar-content atmosphere. They are killed, however, by the 240°F temperatures achieved by heating under pressure.

Pressure-Cooker Canning

Pressure canning is not only a wonderful way to preserve veg-etables, but it's also a great way to preserve meats, poultry, and fish. Modern pressure canners are lightweight, thin-walled alumi-num or stainless-steel kettles. Most have twist-on lids fitted with gaskets. They have removable racks, a weighted vent port (steam vent), and a safety vent. They also have either a dial gauge for indi-cating the pressure or a weighted gauge that rattles when the appro-priate pressure has been reached.

Unlike in a water-bath canner, the jars do not need to be com-pletely covered with water in a pressure canner. The directions that come with your specific brand of pressure canner tell you how many cups of water to add in order for it to generate the right amount of pressure.

Place the specific amount of water into the canner, along with the rack. Place the canner on the burner and bring the water to a boil. Place the filled jars, already fitted with lids, on the rack in the canner. Place the canner lid on the canner and twist to seal it down. Initially leave the pressure weight off the vent port until the water boils and steam escapes strongly from the open vent. Let the steam flow for ten minutes. Place the weight on the vent. Once the pressure gauge has indicated the proper pressure or the weight has begun to rattle, you can start timing your jars according to the recipe you use. Adjust the stove temperature to maintain the desired pressure. Once the time has elapsed, turn the heat off and allow the canner to cool down until the pressure is vented.

Once the canner has cooled, lift off the weight, open the top, and remove the jars. Carefully place the jars onto a towel or wooden board.

Self-Sufficient Facts, Knowledge, and Support
Do not try to open the canner while there is still pressure inside. This can cause a serious scalding.

PRACTICE PICKLING

Pickling is one of the oldest methods of preserving foods and is a process that can be applied to vegetables, meats, eggs, and fruit. Pickling preserves food in an acid, such as vinegar, and this acidic environment prevents growth of undesirable bacteria.

The varieties of pickled and fermented foods are classified by ingredients and method of preparation. Regular dill pickles and sauerkraut are fermented and cured for about three weeks. Refrigerator dills are fermented for about one week. Fresh-pack or quick-process pickles are not fermented; some are brined several hours or overnight, then drained and covered with vinegar and seasonings. Fruit pickles usually are prepared by heating fruit in seasoned syrup acidified with either lemon juice or vinegar. Relishes are made from chopped fruits and vegetables that are cooked with seasonings and vinegar.

 Self-Sufficient Facts, Knowledge, and Support
Most pickled foods are salted or soaked in brine first to draw out moisture that would dilute the acid used to safely preserve the food.

As mentioned before, the safety of canning relies on the acidity of the contents of the jar. The level of acidity in a pickled product is as important to its safety as it is to taste and texture. Make sure you are using vinegar with a 4 to 6 percent acid to be safe, although many food safety professionals are now advising 5 percent. Do not alter vinegar, food, or water proportions in a recipe and do not use vinegar with unknown acidity. Use only recipes with tested proportions of ingredients. Select fresh, unspoiled, and unblemished fruits or vegetables. Use canning or pickling salt. White vinegar is usually preferred when light color is desirable, as is the case with fruits and cauliflower.

PRESERVE WITH FERMENTATION

Fermentation is another ancient and natural form of food preservation, so old that it predates humankind. The basic idea behind fermentation is that you allow food to decay in such a way that it makes a more desirable product. You're probably thinking that you've seen plenty of decayed food, and it didn't seem all that desirable. You'd be right, but just as with so many things, there's good decay and bad decay. Decay is caused by bacteria, so it's not surprising that good decay comes from what are considered to be good bacteria.

Perhaps you've never imagined that you have any relationship with bacteria, but if you've ever eaten any fermented foods, and you surely have, then you've relied on the work of certain bacteria. If you've prepared fermented food, then you've given these bacteria what they wanted, carbohydrates, and they've given you what you wanted, food-preserving acids.

In the fermentation process, the good microbes starve out the bad microbes, which cause the deterioration of food. Fermentation done the right way to the right foods can cause them to remain deliciously edible for years, but most people ferment foods more for the improvements they make to the foods than for the increased shelf life. Bread is fermented for the tangy taste of sourdough; cocoa beans are fermented to improve the taste of chocolate; and yogurt and kefir are fermented to make them tasty and more easily digested.

In fact, fermentation is used in some of your favorite, most sophisticated edibles, such as prosciutto, blue cheese, wine, beer, pickled vegetables, and even butter.

DRY YOUR FOOD

Perhaps the oldest method of preserving food is drying it. Drying is the process of removing water from food to prevent the growth of micro-organisms and decay. Air-drying food is more applicable to people living in a warm and dry climate, but with today's countertop dehydrators, even leftovers can be chopped into smaller pieces, placed into a dryer, and packaged for later.

The quicker the drying can be accomplished, the better the quality of the finished product in both taste and vitamin content. Drying can also be accomplished outdoors in a dry, sunny climate. You can also dry food directly on the racks of your kitchen oven.

Preserve Your Sustainable Lifestyle

When dehydrating food, faster is better, and a higher temperature means drying will take place faster. However, if the temperature is too high, the outside of the fruit or vegetable will dry out and harden faster than the inside, which may not get fully dehydrated and thus spoil in storage.

Drying foods is not as precise as canning and freezing because it involves so many factors, including type of food, water content, climate, and humidity. However, there are some basic guidelines that should be followed:

- Start with fresh, unblemished, unspoiled food.
- Cut food into small, thin slices.
- Place food so it does not overlap.
- Turn food frequently to ensure a consistent dehydration.
- Store dried foods in a closed container at room temperature and use within one year.

You can dry many different kinds of fruits, vegetables, herbs, and meats. You are primarily looking for denser material that does not hold a lot of liquid. For example, watermelon is not a good fruit to dry. It's a good idea to start off with a small batch of whichever food you want to dry to see if you are satisfied with the taste, texture, and color of the finished product.

You might want to see which foods are commercially dried—cherries, apples, herbs, and beef—to give you an idea of some of the things you might want to dry at first. Then feel free to use your knowledge and experiment with other foods, following the appropriate safety standards.

A Quick, Cheap, Homemade Food Dehydrator

If you'd like to try food drying before you commit to the purchase of a dehydrator, you can make a serviceable one without spending a lot of money. To do this, you only need three common items: a window box fan, four paper air-conditioner filters about the same size as the fan (20" × 20"), and two bungee cords. If you buy the cheapest examples of these that you can find, you should be able to get everything for less than $30.

Putting your low-budget dehydrator into operation is the easiest part of the job, much easier even than slicing and preparing the food you want to dry. A very good food to start out with is marinated strips of flank steak. Simply spread out the steak strips on the air-conditioner filters, and stack the filters one on top of the other. Then fix the stack of beef-laden filters to the front (the windy side) of the box fan with the bungee cords and turn it on. Just a few hours later, you will have some of the tastiest beef jerky you've ever eaten.

Drying Fruits and Vegetables

Drying produce is much the same as drying jerky, only it usually doesn't take quite as long. The main caveat is that you need to be careful to slice all the pieces to a uniform thickness so they'll all dry in about the same amount of time. As when freezing, vegetables should be blanched before drying (with some exceptions, such as mushrooms). Fruits, however, need only to be washed, cored, peeled if you desire, and sliced, although you may want to blanch grapes and plums to crack the skins so that the pulp will dry faster.

You'll want to rehydrate most vegetables and some of the fruits that you dry before you use them, unlike the steak jerky. To do this, pour a cup and a half of boiling water over each cup of dried food and let it stand until all the water has been absorbed back into the food. This will take a couple hours for most vegetables, and perhaps overnight for most fruits.

Drying Herbs

This process is so simple that it doesn't require anything other than the herbs you're drying. Pick the herbs just before they blossom in order to get the leaves when they're full of their essential oils. Cut them in the morning as soon as the dew has dried, and try to use only clean plants so that you don't need to wash them, artificially adding to their moisture content. Letting the leaves remain on the stems, bring them indoors and hang them upside down in a warm, dry place with good air circulation and no direct light. This is the best method for drying sage, savory, oregano, basil, marjoram, mint, lemon balm, and horehound. When drying thyme, parsley, lemon verbena, rosemary, and chervil, remove the leaves from the stem and spread them in a single layer on a tray.

USE FREEZING AND COLD STORAGE

Freezing food is an excellent method of food preservation. It allows many foods to be stored for weeks or even months longer than they can be in the refrigerator and to be defrosted as needed, with no or very little loss of quality and nutrients.

Freezing is one of the easiest ways to store food, and also one of the best in terms of retaining the original flavor, but unless you live at the North Pole, freezing costs money because you have to keep the freezer running 24/7 year-round. (Indeed, if you are running a completely off-the-grid home, this may be a difficult—or nearly impossible—task.)

Preserve Your Sustainable Lifestyle

Heavy plastic, aluminum foil, and freezer paper all work suitably to seal the moisture inside the packages. Freezer burn occurs when the meat is allowed to dry out, resulting in loss of taste and color, so it is of the utmost importance that the packages be wrapped airtight to preserve freshness and avoid rancidity. Pork and cured meats should be wrapped in double thickness.

In order to freeze food, you'll need a freezer that's already been brought to the desired low temperature, and you'll need containers. Most any container will do, so long as it will keep the air out and the moisture in. Plastic containers work very well because they can expand as needed when their contents freeze. Metal or glass containers will work also if you leave a little space inside to allow for the expansion of the contents. Plastic bags work nicely because they can be closed as tightly as possible to minimize the air in each package.

Freeze food as quickly as possible after harvest. Never freeze food that has even the smallest degree of spoilage. When freezing nonliquid foods, such as vegetables or loose berries, fill your freezer containers as full as possible, because air dries out food. For example, when freezing blueberries you should clean the berries and air-dry them. Then pack them tightly into containers, being careful not to crush them, but filling the container to capacity. If you're freezing liquids, remember to leave expansion space in the containers. To keep items from freezing into one big block of produce, spread them out on cookie sheets and initially freeze them this way. When frozen, transfer to a container.

Milk

You can freeze milk, whether whole, skimmed, pasteurized, or raw, by pouring it into glass or plastic containers and allowing about 2" of space in the top for expansion. Whole milk can be kept in the freezer for four to five months, but cream shouldn't be kept for more than two or three months. When freezing cream, the butterfat tends to separate, so you can't use it directly, such as on berries or in your coffee, and it may not whip well. Rather, beat it lightly before using and use it for cooking crème sauces, gravies, or custards.

Eggs

Eggs will keep for up to six months in the freezer. Use only the eggs you have gathered that day. Eggs from yesterday or the day before should be eaten fresh and not stored. To freeze eggs, they will need to be shelled first and then you can freeze them whole, or freeze the whites and yolks separately. Whichever way you choose, you'll need to stabilize the yolks so that they don't become hard or thick after they're thawed. Do this by adding 1 teaspoon of salt, or of honey, for each twelve yolks and break and stir the yolks; or, if you're freezing the whole eggs, scramble them together with the salt or honey. Eggs should be thawed completely before using, and use them immediately after thawing.

Self-Sufficient Facts, Knowledge, and Support
When thawing frozen food, as soon as the food reaches 40°F, bacteria that may have been present before freezing starts to grow again. Avoid letting food get that warm before it is thawed. The three safe ways to thaw perishable food are in the refrigerator, in cold water, or in a microwave.

Meat
Freezing is the safest and easiest way to store meat long-term. Having said that, you should not attempt to freeze processed or spiced meats, and cured or smoked meats should not be frozen for longer than two months, because they oxidize more rapidly than fresh-frozen meats. Seasonings limit the freezer life of meats, so if you want to freeze sausage, for example, freeze only the ground meat, and add the seasonings after you thaw the package.

Vegetables
Garden and orchard produce is an excellent candidate for freezing, if the appropriate steps, such as blanching, are taken. Fresh produce contains enzymes that work to destroy the flavors of your food over time, even while they're in storage. These enzymes can survive freezing, but they can't survive high heat, so you'll want to resort to blanching. In this process, the freshly picked produce is quickly scalded with boiling water, or steamed, to kill as many of the enzymes as possible, then just as quickly cooled under cold water before being packed into the freezing containers and stored in the

freezer. For the best results, freeze the produce as soon as possible after harvesting. Any vegetables that are to be cooked before eating will freeze well; those that are generally eaten raw, not so much.

Fruits

Most fruits freeze even better than vegetables because they don't need to be blanched. In fact, fruits frozen properly retain more of their flavor and nutrition than when using any other storage method. You can freeze fruit dry or in a sweet liquid. Dry is acceptable, but fruits will tend to retain more of their flavor, color, and texture if you freeze them in a light syrup. This does not have to be a sugar syrup, which has little or no nutritional value. You can make a light syrup with 1 part mildly flavored honey to 3 parts extremely hot water. Let the syrup cool before adding it to the fruit. You can also add pectin to the syrup, which will retard darkening of the fruit. Fruit should be thawed in its original container and served before it has fully thawed.

Cold Storage

This is one of the oldest and easiest methods of storage, assuming you already have your storage place completed. Many vegetables and some fruits will keep very well for months in cold storage. The basic idea behind cold storage is to keep the foodstuffs you want to carry over the season in a cool, but not freezing, place that has enough moisture to keep the produce from shriveling. Traditionally, this was done in an outdoor root cellar, or if the cellar was under the farmhouse, it would have had a dirt floor that created a nice moist atmosphere, and an outlet to the outdoors to let enough cold in to keep the food cool, but not frozen.

These days, there aren't a lot of root cellars left, and basement floors tend to be paved. If you don't have one of these storage

rooms, you can improvise using containers, crates, or barrels in protected outdoor locations.

Leave Them in the Ground

The simplest way to put root crops into cold storage is to just
leave them in the ground where they grew. Cover them with a mulch
thick enough to keep the ground from freezing. If there's any doubt,
after the mulch has been applied, mark them so that you can find
them later on in the dead of winter. Then dig them up and use them
as needed.

Straw-Bale Root Cellar

Many crops will keep well in proper cold storage, including
apples, pears, grapes, squash, onions, cabbage, celery, garlic, potatoes, and even peppers and tomatoes. You can make a quick, easy,
and affordable place to do your cold storage by building one from
hay or straw bales. Simply place bales on the ground in a square
that leaves a box inside where the produce will be kept, and then
cover the top with a second layer of bales, which will amount to both
the ceiling and the door of your storage space. You can place a brick
or stick of wood under one or two of the top bales to provide ventilation; this should be removed when freezing temperatures prevail.
Some of your produce, such as onions, garlic, and winter squash,
will require curing, which means leaving them in the field to dry out
for a couple weeks after harvesting before you put them in storage.

You shouldn't store apples and potatoes together. Apples produce ethylene gas as they ripen, which can cause the potatoes to
sprout. As if that weren't enough reason, the potatoes will give the
apples a musty flavor. You also shouldn't store onions and potatoes
together because each produces gases that will cause the other to
spoil. You can store produce in containers filled with slightly moist

sand or dry newspapers to keep the individual fruits from touching one another. There are many different ways to keep fruits and vegetables in cold storage, so you will benefit by doing a little research to find out the optimum conditions for the foods you have the most of. A good general rule that applies to all of them is that you should only use your best samples for storing. Bruised or damaged fruit should be eaten fresh.

CURE YOUR MEATS

Curing meats is defined as drying, smoking, adding seasonings or salt, or any combination of these methods. Adding some natural preservatives such as sugar, vinegar, or curing salts may also be involved in the curing process. Curing meat and fish will maintain the quality of the product while allowing it to be stored for a period of time.

Often the curing process involves brine, which is simply a solution of salt and water. The purpose of brine is to draw the natural sugars and moisture from foods and to form the lactic acids that protect the food against spoilage bacteria. Alone, meat is a low-acid food, so be careful to follow the preparation instructions to avoid bacterial growth.

The curing process lengthens the storage life of meats while adding a distinctive flavor. Ham and bacon are the most common cuts of meat cured; however, pork chops, beef ribs, lamb, chicken, and turkey are all tasty when cured.

Be sure, though, that you thoroughly research smoking and curing before attempting them yourself, or better yet, watch and learn from an experienced hand. Meat products are extremely perishable, and nitrates and nitrites used in some curing operations can be toxic to humans in great enough amounts.

CHAPTER 8
Composting

Compost is one of nature's best mulches and soil modifiers. It is cheap, you can use it instead of fertilizers, and it's better for your soil. Compost is the entire basis of organic gardening, and, in a very real way, the basis of all life because every living thing benefits from compost, and every living thing eventually becomes compost. Waste management is a constant part of your self-sufficient lifestyle; composting excess kitchen scraps and waste will help you to fertilize soil and grow crops. Composting is also a great way to go green—rather than hauling waste from your home, yard, or animals to the landfill, you can reuse the materials easily and help reduce your carbon footprint. You can compost kitchen waste, thin layers of lawn clippings, chopped leaves, shredded branches, disease-free garden plants, shredded paper, weeds, straw or hay, newspaper wood ash, and tea leaves. Understanding how composting works, and how you can make it work for you on your own land, will help make a cleaner environment for your home, and all your crops a success.

LEARN THE BASICS OF COMPOSTING

In the simplest terms, composting is the rotting of materials. What makes composting different from simply letting things rot is that by directing the composting process, you can produce a material that is a cure for almost any problem that may arise in plant growth.

Compost is thought of as simply a fertilizer, but it does a great deal more than enrich the soil. Compost can fight the effects of drought by improving your soil's water retention while at the same time combating root flooding and sour soil by improving drainage. Compost applied as mulch can keep your plants cooler on hot summer days and protect roots against deep frost in the winter. Compost added to hard-packed clay soils will make them looser and more arable, and when added to thin, sandy soils, it will make them richer and denser.

When you hear all the virtues of compost and then consider that you can make it yourself for next to nothing, you may start to understand why organic gardeners tend to speak of it in such reverent, respectful terms. If you're not yet convinced, and if you plan to farm at your self-sufficient home, then you need to learn more about how to compost and about what compost can do for you.

Preserve Your Sustainable Lifestyle

Even "finished" compost is only partly decayed. The decomposition continues when the compost is added to your garden soil, which provides food for growing populations of beneficial micro-organisms that convert the compost into dark humus through aerobic and anaerobic breakdown of the various organic materials.

Making compost is one of the easiest things in the world. You just lay any organic substance on the ground and wait; sooner or later it will rot and become compost. The catch is that this method takes a long time and doesn't produce the best compost. In order to speed things up considerably, and to improve the quality of the end product, you'll need to follow certain guidelines.

N-P-K

If you've ever read the wording on a bag of fertilizer, you've seen a series of three numbers, something like 12-10-12. These numbers refer to the analysis of the fertilizer for the three major nutrients plants require—nitrogen, potassium, and phosphorus—by weight. These numbers are always in the same order: N-P-K. So in the example given, a fertilizer with those numbers will contain 12 percent of the weight of the product in nitrogen, 10 percent in potassium, and 12 percent in phosphorus. When you take a soil test of your garden areas, you'll also learn the makeup of these nutrients in your soil. Thus, when you see a deficiency in one or another of them, you'll know that you want to add that element.

Commercial chemical fertilizers provide you with the amount of N-P-K that you want, but add nothing else to the soil, just the chemical. Chemical fertilizers, if applied incorrectly, can burn your plants; even when applied correctly, they do nothing to improve your soil.

When you make compost, the resulting product will also have an N-P-K analysis, but it won't be so constant. The compost will improve your soil in a number of ways other than adding nutrients, and if you've made your compost correctly, you could plant your plants directly into it and they would not burn. By far, the safest and most effective way to improve your garden soil is with composting.

CHOOSE COMPOST INGREDIENTS

Any organic substance will compost, but some of them work better than others. Here's a list of materials that should be fairly easy to find and will work nicely in your pile. A good pile will have twenty-five or thirty times as much carbon as nitrogen. Here are some good, commonly available sources of nitrogen:

■ Brewery waste
■ Cottonseed meal
■ Dried blood (blood meal)
■ Feathers
■ Grass clippings
■ Manure of all kinds. Rabbit manure is one of the best available. Poultry manure tends to be better than that of larger livestock.

Here are some good, commonly available sources of carbon:

■ Cornstalks
■ Dried leaves
■ Pine needles
■ Rotted sawdust
■ Straw

Composting materials are so varied that you shouldn't need to buy anything to start composting. But, if you're just getting started, and you have a whole garden to design and plant and nothing much in the way of compost or soil amendments, you may find it is helpful to buy yourself a truckload of materials to get started.

Many cities now compost the spring yard waste they pick up from citizens, and they make this compost available to the public at reasonable rates. However, if that isn't an option in your neighborhood, look around the outlying area for a turkey or chicken farm. These places tend to have huge, long houses filled with poultry, and they keep the floors of these houses covered with loose materials such as sawdust, rice hulls, and cottonseed hulls, which they refer to as "bedding." They change this bedding with every new crop of birds, and often have a second business selling the used bedding, which is about 50 percent manure. Generally, they'll have a dump truck and will deliver a whole truckload of the stuff to your backyard for a very reasonable rate.

When it gets there, it'll be in fine shape: loose, dry, and in reasonably small particles so you can treat it as a readymade compost pile. Dump it in an appropriate spot, wet it down, and start adding your own kitchen garbage and other compostable finds to it regularly while turning it often. You can use it sparingly as a side dressing (at this stage, it can burn your plants if you use too much), or just let the whole thing sit for a few months. Either way, you'll end up with a lot of good compost as easily and quickly as any other method you'll find.

AVOID HAZARDOUS MATERIALS

Nearly anything can go into a compost pile, but there are a few things that you should avoid using, or be especially careful when you do. Obviously, you don't want to add anything to the pile that may be poisonous to plants, and some materials, such as materials that contain metals, can carry hidden dangers. You also don't want to add materials that might prove to be nutritious to your plants eventually but take too long to break down, perhaps causing deficiencies in the short term. Nor do you want to include matter that might be dangerous to human health or could draw rodents or carrion-eaters to rummage through the pile.

- Green sawdust. Green sawdust, sawdust from unseasoned wood, is very slow to decompose, and it can suck the nitrogen out of your pile as it does. A compost pile can break down green sawdust if there's plenty of nitrogen and not too much sawdust, but you'll spend your efforts better using well-rotted sawdust instead. You can find well-rotted sawdust at sawmills, horse barns, and composted yard clippings. (It is usually black in appearance.) You can also make your own; it generally takes two to four years to break down.
- Newsprint and coated paper. These are sometimes difficult to chop into fine pieces, and some inks are toxic to plants. If you use papers, make certain that they have been cut up as fine as confetti and make certain you use lots of nitrogen.
- Human or carnivorous animal feces. Like used personal products, these present too many health risks. Blood and manure from noncarnivorous animals is excellent, however.
- Walnut leaves or residue. Alone, walnut products will fertilize a pasture, but don't use them in the compost pile. They contain juglone, a natural compound that is toxic to several plants.
- Large lumps of anything edible. Your compost pile will certainly swallow up garbage in time, but the bigger the pieces are, the more likelihood that you'll have neighborhood animals turning the pile for you, and they don't do a very neat or thorough job. They just dig out the goodies that they like, and perhaps spread parts of them on the ground outside the

pile as they dine. Many experts will advise you against including anything edible in the compost pile, because it will draw rodents and other pests. However, if the material is finely chopped and mixed into the amalgam, and you can keep the critters at bay, most foodstuffs will produce a potent compost.

BUILD A SMALL PILE FOR YOUR HOME

As already mentioned, compost can be made from any once-living thing. However, to make potent compost quickly, you need to concentrate on two things: the physical size of the particles and the nitrogen content of the materials you use. Before you add a material to your compost pile, it needs to be chopped into fine particles of less than ½" or so in diameter. If doing this by hand is too tedious, a wood chipper works superbly. If you don't have a wood chipper, you can get similar results by running a lawn mower over your materials, a bit at a time, until they are ground up.

Grinding or chopping makes the ingredients loose and easy to turn and allows oxygen into the depths of the material. Oxygen is necessary for the composting process.

The materials you use can be anything you have a surplus of, but it's important that you add an abundance of nitrogen-rich compounds to the mix. That's because nitrogen will produce heat in the compost pile, and that heat speeds up the composting process. Materials commonly used that are "hot" (high in nitrogen) include manures, grass clippings, kitchen waste, and green vegetable matter such as weeds.

Once your ingredients are chopped or ground, it's time to place them on the pile. Layering each material is a good way to make

certain that the different substances are distributed evenly throughout the pile, and adding a layer of good soil to every third or fourth
layer of other materials will introduce new organisms into the batch.
Once you've built your pile up to a depth of 3 to 5 feet, sprinkle it
thoroughly with a garden hose and leave it to stand for a few days.

Preserve Your Sustainable Lifestyle

Building a compost pile is the intensification and
optimization of a natural process that goes on everywhere all the time. When a lawn is mowed, when
autumn leaves fall to the ground, when insects, animals, and all living things die, these organic substances revert to humus through the composting
process.

Remember that if your pile is too small, it won't heat up and thus
won't compost. You want it to be 3 to 5 feet deep and at least that
much in diameter.

Self-Sufficient Facts, Knowledge, and Support

Always locate a new compost pile on bare, rock-free
ground. If the pile is placed on concrete, worms and
beneficial microorganisms can't enter the pile from
the soil below. If the soil below the pile is rocky,
you're likely to wind up with some of these rocks in
the garden.

During cold weather you may look out the window on a frosty
morning and see steam wafting from your compost pile. This is

good, as it shows that the pile is heating up. After a few days, it will be time to turn the pile.

Heating Up

If you have a small pile, shovel it all from one spot to another. As you do this, you should notice that the pile is still steaming slightly and is warm, or even hot, to the touch. There'll be an abundance of gray flecks in the material inside the pile. This is ash, and it shows you that the pile is heating up and speeding decomposition of the various ingredients. If you don't see these gray flecks, check to make certain that the pile is not too wet or too dry (it should be moist but not soggy), that your materials are thoroughly chopped, and that the nitrogen source is evenly distributed throughout the pile in sufficient amounts. After you've turned the pile, it should start to heat up again, but not so much as at first. After a third turning with successful heating, you can be assured you have finished compost.

Once you have a compost pile "cooking," it will initially heat up to more than 150°F (66°C), which will kill most harmful bacteria and weed seeds, so don't worry about putting it on your garden. You can make compost out of anything, but you want to make certain that your compost is rich in all the essential nutrients. Here are some facts and suggestions about what these nutrients are and how to get them:

■ N=Nitrogen: Ideally, you've already supplied a nice base of nitrogen-rich materials to your pile. Besides causing the pile to heat up, nitrogen is extremely important to plant growth because it promotes leaf and stem development and provides the energy to set fruit and develop seeds. In short, nitrogen is directly responsible for the vegetative growth of plants above ground. When you see a plant with pale green or yellow leaves and lackluster growth, this is a sign of nitrogen deficiency. Too much nitrogen can result in excessive dark-green growth, but nitrogen excess is not commonly a problem, especially if your nitrogen has gone through the composting process; it occurs more routinely when chemical fertilizers are used. Rich nitrogen sources include manure, blood, hair, grass clippings, kitchen waste, and green vegetable matter.

- P=Potassium: Potassium, or potash, increases plants' resistance to disease, heat, and cold. Potassium can even help plants overcome a nitrogen excess. Potash deficiencies result in sickly, purplish plants with weak stems, slow growth, and few blossoms or fruits. You can't see it, of course, but their photosynthesis has slowed down. One of the best and least-expensive sources of potash is wood ash (from a wood fire). Ashes from deciduous trees are better than from conifers, but they're both loaded with the stuff, and it's ready for the compost pile as soon as you get it—no preparation is necessary.

- K=Phosphorus: Phosphates are essential to the development of strong, healthy roots. Whenever you see a commercial fertilizer promoted as a "bloom booster" or something of that sort, it is because a high percentage of phosphorus is present. In addition, phosphorus also promotes disease resistance and fruit development. Soils that are low in humus—the dark, organic material in soil produced by decomposition—are also low in phosphorus. If you suspect that your plants aren't getting enough phosphorus, an excellent source is bone meal, but good compost will contain all you need in a typical application. Weak plants that seem to attract insect damage and have thin-skinned fruits suggest a deficiency in phosphorus.

Secondary Nutrients

In addition to N, P, and K, plants need many other nutrients, but usually in such small amounts that enough of them are present in the soil without amendments. Some of these nutrients include calcium, magnesium, and sulfur. If you add lime to your soil to adjust the pH, this lime will contain all the calcium and magnesium you need. Sulfur is found in decomposing organic matter, so your compost pile has plenty already.

APPLY COMPOST TO YOUR SOIL

If your compost is thoroughly chopped and completely finished, you can apply it directly to the garden. It's best to do this right after you've tilled the area to loosen the soil, and then apply 3" or 4" of compost on top and stir it around to mix it with the loose soil below. Ideally, you will do this a month or so before you plant.

Preserve Your Sustainable Lifestyle

If the pile is no longer heating, and you can't recognize any of the original elements, then it's probably finished. If in doubt, put soggy compost into a jar. If it smells bad after a week, it's not finished. If it has an earthy smell, it's ready for the garden.

If, for whatever reason, you have some not-yet-finished compost, you can apply this to a section of garden in the late fall, or a few months before you expect to plant, and the decomposition will complete in the ground.

You can fertilize when your plants are already in the ground by placing the compost on top of the soil beside the plants—what's known as "side-dressing"—or better yet, by mixing the compost with some loose topsoil and using the combination as a thick mulch. In this way, you fertilize the plants as the nutrients work their way down to the roots. Meanwhile, your plants will enjoy the benefits of a thick mulch: protection from hard rains and erosion, moderation of soil temperatures, and discouragement of weeds.

Don't worry about applying too much compost. Plants will grow in pure compost, although they need soil to do their best. If you have enough compost to apply 3" to 6" a year, your soil and your plants will benefit from it.

BUILD A COMPOST ENCLOSURE

Your compost pile doesn't really need to be enclosed at all. You'll be more proud of it than ashamed, and it really isn't unattractive; it's just a brown mound in the backyard. However, you may wish to build some sort of enclosure, and having your materials closed in may make it a little easier when it's time to turn them. In any case, if you do build an enclosure, be sure that one whole end, not just a door, opens to make it easier to access and turn. Building the enclosure out of some perforated or open material, such as picket fencing or chicken wire, will assure that plenty of air can get into the back and sides of the pile. Some folks build two bins side by side, and when it comes time to turn the pile, they shovel the contents of the first bin into the second one.

You also may choose to enclose your compost pile to keep pests out of it. That may mean putting some sort of lid over it that will let the rain in and keep the varmints out, in addition to enclosing the four sides.

Self-Sufficient Facts, Knowledge, and Support
Dying plant and animal residues is what makes "living" soil. An acre of healthy soil contains thousands of pounds of actinomycetes bacteria, fungi, protozoans, yeasts, algae, earthworms, and insects performing different roles but working together in the process of converting dead material into humus.

If you build an enclosure that can be easily lifted away when you want to work on the pile, this may present the best of both worlds. If you have a larger pile on a larger lot, you may start using your skid loader or tractor loader to turn the pile or to scoop out a bucketful to take to the garden. If so, you'll want to be able to move any enclosures you've built out of harm's way until the job is finished.

TROUBLESHOOT ANY COMPOSTING ISSUES

There are a few common problems that folks encounter when building a compost pile. If you follow the instructions here, you aren't likely to encounter any of them, but in case you do, here's a troubleshooter guide.

Pile Too Wet

If you're experiencing a long period of rainy weather, put a tarp over the pile and let it dry out a bit. If you suspect that the problem isn't the weather, perhaps you added some thick, matting material such as leaves to the pile without chopping it up. If that's the case, you may need to either pull out the offending material, let it dry, and chop it up, or just wait a long while; it will compost anaerobically . . . eventually.

Self-Sufficient Facts, Knowledge, and Support
Covering the pile should only be done on a temporary basis to remedy too much moisture or to control odors in the short term while the pile adjusts itself. All other times, it should be left open to the elements where it can take in rain and oxygen.

Pile Too Dry

It's hard to imagine this happening in any part of the world that has regular rainfall, but if you live in a desert or are experiencing a long drought, your compost may dry out too much. If that's the case, all you need to do is soak it down with a hose or sprinkler. Compost should be uniformly moist, but not soggy.

Pile Smells Bad

Most likely your pile isn't aerating properly. Perhaps some of the materials are not chopped enough and are bunching up, in which case the solution may be as simple as turning the pile. If that doesn't work, you may need to break down any matted materials. It's also possible that the pile may just be too wet. If it smells like ammonia, that's a sign that you have too much nitrogen-laden material. Try adding something less hot, such as rotten sawdust, rice hulls, or even garden soil.

Bugs, Flies, Worms

Follow the instructions for a too-wet pile, and try adding some drier material, such as chopped hay or straw. If the pile isn't heating, then add nitrogen and turn it again.

CHAPTER 9
Beekeeping

People have been keeping bees for more than 150 years. It is unlikely that you will find smaller livestock than honeybees, and pound-for-pound (or gram-for-gram) you'll also have trouble finding more profitable creatures for your self-sufficient home. Bees are an essential part of agriculture, necessary for pollinating plants to ensure a better fruit set and bigger crops. If you decide to keep bees as a part of your self-sufficient lifestyle, you'll find your plants and crops will produce more fruits with higher seed yields, and you'll see a direct impact on the quality of crops you harvest. Beekeeping is one of the few farm activities that can actually increase yields rather than simply protect existing yields from losses. Once you establish your beehives, you'll also reap the benefits of a delectable and versatile honey crop year after year.

LEARN THE LEGAL REQUIREMENTS

All states have laws that pertain to keeping bees and registering hives. You need to understand the laws of your state before you begin beekeeping. Now, because of parasitic bee mites and the Africanized honeybee, some states have even more stringent laws. For specific legal information, you can contact your county extension agent or your state department of agriculture.

Self-Sufficient Facts, Knowledge, and Support
Bees pollinate about one-sixth of the world's flowering plant species and some 400 of its agricultural plants.

FIGURE OUT IF YOUR AREA IS RIGHT FOR BEEKEEPING

Honeybees can be kept almost anywhere there are flowering plants that produce nectar and pollen. Choose a site for beehives that is discrete, sheltered from winds, and partially shaded. Avoid low spots in a yard where cold, damp air accumulates in winter.

The best beehive location is one where your best source of pollen and nectar is within two square miles of your hive; the closer the better. Because bees actually use pollen and nectar to produce their own energy, the farther they have to travel for it, the more they have to consume themselves. If you can place them closer to their food source, you can collect more honey.

The best position for a hive is where it will also have afternoon shade, shielding the hive from the summer sun. Shade, rather than sunlight, will give the bees more time to concentrate their effort on making honey, because they won't need to work at carrying water back and forth to cool the hive.

BUY BASIC BEEKEEPING EQUIPMENT

A manmade hive is built to imitate the space that bees leave between their honeycombs in nature. The dimensions are fairly standard and should be copied exactly if you decide to make your own beehives. The following equipment is used within a hive:

- Bottom board: a wooden stand that the hive rests upon. Bottom boards can be set on bricks, concrete blocks, cinder blocks, or any stable base to keep the hive off the ground.
- Hive body or brood super: a large wooden box that holds eight to ten frames of comb. In this space, the bees rear their brood and store honey for their own use. Up to three brood supers can be used for a brood nest.
- Frames and foundation: frames hang inside each super or box on a specially cut ledge called a rabbet. Frames keep the combs organized inside your hive and allow you to easily and safely inspect your bees. Frames hold thin sheets of beeswax foundation, which is embossed with the shapes of hexagonal cells. Foundations help bees to build straight combs.
- Queen excluder: a frame made with wire mesh placed between the brood super and the honey super, sized so workers can move between the brood super and the honey super but keeps the queen in the brood super so brooding will not occur in honey supers.

- Honey supers: shallow boxes with frames of comb hanging in them for bees to store surplus honey. The honey supers hold the honey that is harvested from the hive.
- Inner cover: placed on top of the honey super to prevent bees from attaching comb to the outer cover. It also provides insulating dead air space.
- Outer cover: placed on top of the hive to provide weather protection.

Preserve Your Sustainable Lifestyle

Generally, you need light-colored over-gear to keep your clothes clean and to create a barrier between you and the bees. Bees are not threatened by light colors, so the color of the suit makes a great difference as to whether the bees will attack or not.

The following equipment is personal gear:

- Ankle protection: elastic straps with hook-and-loop attachment to prevent bees from crawling up your pant leg.
- Bee suit or jacket, veil, gloves, and gauntlet: protective personal gear worn when working with bees. Thin, plastic-coated canvas gloves, rather than the stiff, heavy leather commercial gloves, are supple and allow you more movement. Gauntlets are long cuffs that slide over your gloves to keep bees from climbing up your sleeves.
- Feeders: hold sugar syrup that is fed to bees in early spring and in fall.

- Hive tool: looks like a small crowbar. It is ideally shaped for prying apart supers and frames.
- Smoker: a beekeeper's best friend. A smoker calms bees and reduces stinging. Pine straw, sawdust, chipped wood mulch, grass, and burlap make good smoker fuel.

Keep in mind that the proper safety equipment allows you to take care of your bees calmly, and without the fear of being stung. When you're calm and focused, you'll create, nurture, and maintain a successful hive—safely and efficiently.

Preserve Your Sustainable Lifestyle
Don't be surprised if you don't have a honey crop the first year. It's more important that your hive or hives be allowed to put away honey for winter and maintain a strong, vibrant colony. There's always next year.

Avoid Purchasing Used Hives

It is very tempting to buy used hives, but if you do so, do this in the presence of an experienced beekeeper, because used equipment can carry with it contamination by American foulbrood (AFB). AFB is a bacterial contamination of beehives that quickly destroys the entire brood. Bee larvae ingest the spore-forming bacteria, and these bacteria then germinate in the entrails of the larvae, killing them as they release up to one hundred million spores per individual. These spores can survive for more than forty years in honey and beekeeping equipment. The accepted and reliable way to eradicate

AFB is by gamma irradiation. If you're just starting out, it's much simpler to start with new boxes and equipment.

PURCHASE BEES

Usually the best way to start keeping bees is to buy established colonies from a local beekeeper. Often a local beekeeper might even have a colony he or she wants to give away. It's better to get two colonies at the beginning, because this allows you to interchange frames of both brood and honey if one colony becomes weaker than the other and needs a boost.

Have the beekeeper open the supers. The bees should be calm and numerous enough that they fill most of the spaces between combs.

Moving a hive is a two-person job. It's easiest to move a hive during the winter when they are lighter and populations are low. The first thing you want to do is close the hive entrance. You can accomplish this with a piece of folded window screen. Then look for any other cracks and seal them with duct tape. Make sure the supers are fastened together and the bottom board is stapled to the last super. Remember to open hive entrances after the hives are relocated.

Installing Packaged Bees

You can also buy packaged bees and queens. Bees are commonly shipped in 2- to 5-pound packages of about 10,000 to 20,000 bees. Keep the packages cool and shaded when they arrive. To transfer bees to their new hive, set up a bottom board with one hive body and remove half of the frames. Spray the bees heavily with sugar syrup (one part sugar to one part water) through the screen on the package; the bees will gorge themselves with syrup and become sticky, making them easy to pour.

The next step is to move the queen, which will be in a separate cage. Pry off the package lid, remove the can of syrup provided for transit, find and remove the queen suspended in her cage, and reclose the package.

Self-Sufficient Facts, Knowledge, and Support

The queen cage has holes at both ends plugged with cork. Under the cork at one end you will see that it is filled with white "queen candy." Remove the cork from this end and suspend the queen cage between two center frames in your hive. Worker bees will eventually eat through the candy and release the queen.

Shake the original package lightly to move all bees into a pile on the bottom. Take the lid off the package again and pour the bees into the hive on top of the queen. As they slowly spread throughout the hive, carefully return the frames to their original positions. Replace the inner and outer covers on the hive. You have successfully created your first colony. You must now feed the bees sugar water until natural nectar starts to appear.

MANAGE YOUR BEEHIVE

You want your bees to be at their maximum strength before the nectar flow begins. This way, the created honey is stored for harvest rather than used to build up their strength. Feeding and medicating your bees should be done January through February. Because the queens will resume egg-laying in January, some colonies will need supplemental feeding of sugar syrup.

By mid-February, you should inspect your hives. You should be looking for population growth, the arrangement of the brood nest, and disease symptoms. If one of your colonies has less brood than average, you can strengthen it by transferring a frame of sealed brood from your other colony.

If you use two brood supers and find that most of the bees and brood are in the upper super, reverse the supers, placing the top one on the bottom. You want to do this because it relieves congestion. When a colony feels congested it swarms, looking for another place to live. If you only have one brood super, you will need to relieve congestion by providing additional honey supers above a queen excluder.

Annual requeening can be done in early spring or in the fall. Most beekeepers feel that requeening is one of the best investments you can make. Young queens not only lay eggs more prolifically, but they also secrete higher levels of pheromones, which stimulate the worker bees to forage.

In order to requeen a colony, you must find, kill, and discard the old queen. Then you need to allow the colony to remain queenless for twenty-four hours. After that period of time, you can introduce the new queen in her cage, allowing the workers to eat through the candy in order to release her.

By mid-April your colonies should be strong enough to collect surplus nectar. This is when you should add honey supers above the hive bodies. Add enough supers to accommodate both the incoming nectar and the large bee population. Adding supers stimulates foraging and limits late-season swarming.

During late summer and early autumn, the brood production and the honey production drop. At this point, you should crowd the bees by giving them only one or two honey supers. This forces bees to store honey in the brood nest to strengthen the hive. Colonies are usually overwintered in two hive bodies or in one hive body and at least one honey super. Be sure that if you overwinter in one hive body and a honey super, you remove the queen excluder so the queen can move up into the honey super during winter. If your colony is light on stores, feed them heavy syrup (two parts sugar to one part water). Bees should have between 50 and 60 pounds of stores going into winter. A hive with a full deep frame weighs 6 pounds and full shallow frame weighs 3 pounds. You can pick up the frame to estimate the weight of the hive and stores. Never allow stores to drop below 12 to 18 pounds.

COLLECT HONEY

It's best to harvest your honey on a sunny, windless day, as bees are calmest then. Remove the bees from the hive by blowing smoke into the hive opening. After a few minutes, pry the outer cover loose and lift it off. Blow more smoke through the hole in the inner cover. Now you can remove the inner cover. After the inner cover is removed, once again blow smoke into the hive to finally drive the bees downward and out of the way.

Remove the super and pry the frames loose with the hive tool. Be careful not to crush any bees. A crushed bee releases a scent that stimulates other bees to attack. Gently brush off any bees that are clinging to the frames. A comb that is ready to be harvested should be about 80 percent sealed over.

Uncap the combs in a bee-proof location, such as a tightly screened room. Bees will want to take the honey if they can get to it. Slice off the comb tops with a sharp knife warmed in hot water.

A heavy kitchen knife is fine. It's best to use two knives, cutting with one while the other is heating. Once the honey is extracted, return the emptied combs to the hive for the bees to clean and use again. With care, combs can be recycled for twenty years or more.

Self-Sufficient Facts, Knowledge, and Support
Although there are other species of insects that pollinate plants, bees are the only ones that can be moved from place to place and generally manipulated by humans to pollinate crops when and where they choose. That's why many domesticated crops rely solely on the honeybee.

KNOW THE MOST COMMON BEEKEEPING ISSUES

The common problems you encounter when raising bees are swarming, stings, and diseases and pests that can affect your hive. In addition, your neighbors may have a problem with your new hives, no matter how much you assure them of their safety. Some of the most common problems include:

Swarming
You cannot always prevent bees from swarming. You can, however, make a swarm less likely by requeening your colony with a younger queen. You can also have a "bait hive" in place in case a swarm occurs. Bees will cluster within 100 feet of their old hive while the scout bees search for a new hive. A bait hive is simply an attractive home waiting for a swarm to discover.

Stings

If you keep bees, you are going to get stung. You can reduce stinging greatly by taking precautions and wearing protective gear, using a smoker, and handling bees gently. However, the likelihood is that you're still going to get stung. If there is a chance you are allergic to bee stings, you do not want to keep bees. If you are not allergic, you probably will find, as most beekeepers do, that although stings still hurt, after a few stings you generally have less of a reaction.

Honeybee Diseases and Pests

Honeybee brood and adults are attacked by bacteria, viruses, protozoans, fungi, and exotic parasitic mites. Additionally, bees and beekeeping equipment are attacked by a variety of insects. Some insects, including the wax moth, lay eggs on the equipment and their larvae gnaw boat-shaped indentations in the wooden frame or hive body to attach their silken cocoons. With heavy infestations, frame pieces may be weakened to the point of collapse. Some insects, such as spiders, actually eat bees. Disease and pest control requires constant vigilance by the beekeeper. Contact local beekeepers to learn about the diseases and issues prevalent in your area and how to prevent and cure them.

Fearful Neighbors

Bees will not attack humans unless they feel that they need to protect their hive. Unfortunately, if you have any neighbors who are afraid of bees (*apiphobic*), this argument won't likely reassure them. Remember, however, that people keep bees even in the largest cities, and there are solutions to the problem of neighbors. Keeping your hives behind a high wall not only obscures them from sight, but it also forces the bees to fly higher overhead, and above the heads of people in the area.

Bees can be a nuisance around swimming pools and other sources of water because bees use quite a lot of water themselves. This problem can be remedied by providing a plentiful supply of water near the hive. A good apiary site will be hidden, yet exposed to full sunlight with water close by, and be in close proximity to as many flowering plants as possible.

CHAPTER 10
Essential Household Skills

When it comes to living self-sufficiently, you must have a diverse set of skills. A working knowledge of water management, storing foods, and processing animals can make the difference between a comfortable, independent home and a home that is completely unsustainable—or one that is totally dependent on outside systems. The skills and knowledge provided in previous chapters should give you a broad basis from which to build your own self-sufficient lifestyle; however, the tips and guidance in this chapter will help solidify your independence and establish a well-rounded, self-sufficient home, season to season and year after year.

HARVEST AND STORE WATER

Harvesting rainwater is one of the oldest known methods of capturing and storing water to use for irrigating your garden or supplying your household or your livestock with water. These methods are still used by many people in developing nations and are growing more common in the United States, especially in the Southwest, where water is very scarce.

When you are living in a self-sufficient home, you need to think of supplying water for more than just household purposes; you also need to think about extra water for fire protection or emergencies. And, if you have livestock, you need to be sure you have enough water to care for them as well.

The basic foundation of a water harvesting system is the means to direct rainfall where you want it to go. Water harvest can entail a series of small trenches or contoured areas that begin just below the downspouts of your house or your barn and run into your garden. Or, it can be a more sophisticated system with water running from your downspout into some kind of storage container for future use.

Self-Sufficient Facts, Knowledge, and Support
The average American household consumes about 127,400 gallons of water during a year. Homeowners in Washington, DC, pay about $350 for that amount of water. Buying that same amount from a vendor in Guatemala City would cost more than $1,700.

Your roof is not the only surface or "catchment" that can capture rainfall. Any large surface that can capture and/or carry water to where it can be used or stored is also considered a catchment. Think about the catchments on your property—the barn roof, the outhouse roof, the patio, or even the driveway. All of these hard surfaces allow water to run off and have the potential of being part of your water harvest system.

Not all of these catchments have to direct water to the same place. Your roof could have a system that directs the water to barrels attached to your downspouts. Your driveway could have a series of dikes, berms, or contouring to direct the water to irrigate your garden.

Planning Your System

In order to determine how you should store your water, you need to develop a site plan. Using graph paper, draw a scale model of your property with the location of your house, outbuildings, and any other areas that you think might be catchments. Then indicate water flow by drawing arrows to indicate water flow direction across each surface; i.e., your roof will have arrows from the peak going down each side. Add to the drawing those areas that will need water, such as your garden, your livestock area, and your orchard, and even areas in your house that could use graywater, such as your toilets.

Now you can calculate the approximate amount of water you will harvest with the designated catchments. Using your graph paper, calculate the number of square feet in each catchment area. The next thing you need to do is determine the runoff coefficient for the different surfaces of your catchment. The runoff coefficient roughly calculates the percentage of water that will not be absorbed or evaporated from the surface. If the surface is smooth, use the higher coefficient from the following list; if the surface is rough, the lower one. For example, the runoff coefficient for a smooth metal roof is 0.95. Here is a list of the runoff coefficients:

- Gravel: high coefficient 0.70, low coefficient 0.25
- Lawns: flat, sandy soil—high coefficient 0.10, low coefficient 0.05
- Lawns: flat, heavy soil—high coefficient 0.17, low coefficient 0.13

- Paving: concrete, asphalt—high coefficient 1.00, low coefficient 0.90
- Roof: metal, gravel, asphalt, shingle, fiberglass, mineral paper—high coefficient 0.95, low coefficient 0.90
- Soil: flat, bare—high coefficient 0.75, low coefficient 0.20
- Soil: flat, with vegetation—high coefficient 0.60, low coefficient 0.10

With all of this information in hand, you can use the formula that follows to calculate your water capture:

A = average monthly rainfall amount (this can vary greatly from month to month, so you may need to calculate each month's potential water capture)

B = 0.623 (converts inches into gallons per square foot)

C = square footage of the catchment surface

D = the runoff coefficient from the preceding list

$A \times B \times C \times D$ = monthly yield of harvested water in gallons

Once you have calculated the monthly yield from your catchment surfaces, you can determine where you want the water to go.

Preparing Your Site

Your potential harvested water needs somewhere to go. Do you want to divert it all into the garden or orchard? Do you want to store it in holding tanks near your home? Or, do you want to build a cistern and store the water there? These are the next decisions you have to make.

Keep in mind that you need to size your storage container(s) large enough to hold your calculated supply. Water collected from any catchment area can be distributed anywhere on your property through a series of PVC pipes and hoses. However, it will save you time, effort, and money if you are able to locate water storage *close* to the areas needing water, and *higher* than the area to take advantage of gravity flow.

If you live in an area that has minimal rainfall, there are some things you can do to optimize your water harvest:

- Create depressions around trees and line them with rocks or mulch to retain moisture.
- Dig furrows and channels to direct water to a garden.
- If you are designing a new home site for water harvesting, arrange brick or flagstone paving to direct water to plants.
- Make sure your gutters and downspouts are free of trash, dirt, and leaves.

Once you know where your water is going, you need to know how to store it for future use.

Storing Rainwater

Having water surplus available to you at the right time of year makes storage well worth the time and effort. But when water is stored for more than several months, it can stagnate and present a health hazard because it could become a breeding area for mosquitoes.

To determine whether storage should be part of your harvesting system, compare the total amount of water available in a given month (estimated rainfall) to the estimated water usage in the same month. If you find that you have a surplus that can be used in a reasonable amount of time, you should consider a storage system.

A Simple Storage System

You can create a simple water storage system consisting of a plastic barrel placed on a raised platform under a rain-gutter downspout. There should be an opening on top of the barrel for the water to be fed in through the downspout and some kind of filtering system above the opening. The barrel should also have an external pipe with a shutoff valve to control the amount of water withdrawn. If you have designed your system properly, gravity will enable you to send water from the barrel to a drip irrigation system without a pump.

Long-Term Storage Plans

Your water storage plans should be based on having enough water to supply each person with 1 gallon per day. This amount is only for general drinking purposes. You should store more water for cooking and hygiene. If you are able to have a 150-gallon water tank or a number of 50-gallon water barrels, you would be able to serve the basic needs of a family of four for about a month. If you want to store more than one month's worth of water, you will need to multiply the number of containers.

Often you can find used plastic 50-gallon barrels for a reduced price through soft-drink bottlers, who use the barrels for concentrated syrup. You would have to thoroughly clean the buckets to remove the lingering taste, but they would offer you an inexpensive way to store water for your family.

For long-term water storage, tap water should be chemically disinfected by treating each gallon with sixteen drops ($\frac{1}{8}$ teaspoon) of liquid chlorine bleach containing 4 percent to 6 percent sodium hypochlorite. Scented bleach will perfume the water, so don't use it. One teaspoon of bleach disinfects 5 gallons of water. Three tablespoons will disinfect 55 gallons. If you add this to your water, you will kill bacteria and viruses and prevent the growth of micro-organisms during storage.

USE GRAYWATER

The term "graywater" is used when you are talking about water that has already been used once. This doesn't include water from the toilet, which is known as "blackwater," but does include water from the sink, the washing machine, the shower, and the bathtub. Graywater comprises about 50 to 80 percent of all residential water use.

Graywater systems are used for several reasons:

- To promote a green lifestyle by using fewer resources
- To conserve water in an arid area
- To place less stress on a septic system
- To save money, when the cost of pumping water is more expensive than the cost of reusing water

When you build a graywater system, you separate the graywater from the blackwater and send the graywater through a separate treatment system. Blackwater will go into your septic system and graywater will pass through a filtering or purification system. Ideally, after the graywater passes through a purification process, it can then be reused. Graywater systems are particularly appropriate in off-grid locations. They reduce use of fresh water, place less stress on existing conventional septic tanks, have a highly effective purification process, and reduce chemical and energy use.

If you create a system that will separate blackwater from graywater, the graywater can be recycled back into the home and garden. Graywater can be used to flush toilets or irrigate the garden.

Although some systems filter graywater enough to purify it to a state of drinking water, most graywater systems do not allow that degree of filtering. For that reason, graywater should not be used for drinking, cooking, or cleaning.

Preserve Your Sustainable Lifestyle

If you plan on using graywater for irrigation, avoid using laundry powders. These powders often contain high levels of salt as a bulking agent, and this has the same effect on your soil as a drought. Use an organic liquid laundry detergent instead.

Because graywater still carries particles from food, your skin, and cleaning agents, and is often discharged warm, it is important not to store it before using it for irrigation purposes. Storing graywater would allow bacteria to grow in the water and be transferred to your plants.

There are many ways you can filter graywater. The systems that allow you to feed the water back into the home for use in toilet flushing are more complex than those that simply filter the graywater and pressurize it for irrigation purposes. Some building designs, such as Earthship's, include an entire graywater system in their blueprints.

MAINTAIN A SEPTIC SYSTEM

If your home is not connected to a town sewer system, you will need a septic system. Whether or not you decide to recycle graywater, you will still need a septic system to get rid of the blackwater from your home.

There are four main components to a typical septic system:

1. A pipe to carry the waste from the home
2. The actual septic tank to start the digestion process
3. The drain field to spread out the wastewater
4. The soil with microbes to do the final filtering and cleaning of the water

Once the used water enters the system, the pipe carries the water and accompanying waste out of your home and into the working parts of your septic system. The septic tank is actually a watertight tank that is buried several feet underground. Septic tanks have concrete manhole-sized lids that generally sit at ground level, providing easy access for cleaning, inspection, and pumping the tanks.

Tanks can be made of concrete, fiberglass, or polyethylene. When wastewater comes into the tank, the solids settle to the bottom. This material is known as sludge. The oil, grease, and other nonsolid components rise to the top and are known as scum. This separation allows for a partial decomposition of the solid material. This decomposition is aided by a variety of different bacteria and enzymes that naturally break down the human waste in the tank and help it dissolve back into the earth, so you are not just accumulating a massive amount of refuse.

Sludge and scum are prevented from leaching out of the septic tank by a T-shaped outlet design that holds in the more solid materials and allows the water to seep into the drain field. You should use additional screens throughout the system to ensure that the solids do not make it into the drain field.

Once wastewater has been separated from the solids, it exits the septic tank into a drain field to complete its treatment in the soil.

Wastewater is fed into the drain field every time new blackwater and graywater are introduced into the tank.

Self-Sufficient Facts, Knowledge, and Support
The risk of death of beneficial bacterial colonies in your septic tank can be lessened by changing from potent chemical cleaners to organic cleaning products, which are not quite as harsh on the bacteria that work in the tank.

The soil surrounding the drain field is essential in removing contaminants from your wastewater before it is returned to the groundwater. The microbes in the soil remove harmful bacteria, viruses, and nutrients from the wastewater. This is accomplished by the wastewater filtering through the drain field.

Have your soil tested to be sure it is porous enough to allow natural filtration. Once installed, your septic system should be inspected every three years and pumped out every three to five years. However, maintenance of the septic system should be an ongoing process.

Unfortunately, the bacteria and enzymes that eat away the sludge and scum are easily destroyed by bleach or paint thinner entering the system. You can restore the natural enzymes in the system quickly and inexpensively. All you have to do is buy a box or package of the enzymes made for septic systems and flush it down one of the toilets in your home. Some people have found that adding brown sugar with the enzymes helps to increase their viability. You should add enzymes to stimulate the function of your septic tank about once a month for optimal performance.

LEARN TO PROCESS POULTRY

Most poultry can be processed in similar ways. You will find that the biggest differentiating factor is size. A duck can probably be butchered by the same process as a chicken; however, when you are dealing with turkeys and geese, you need to consider their weight and size.

You need to "starve" your birds for up to twenty-four hours before you butcher them. This way their intestines are fairly empty, so there is less chance of contamination when you are processing them. You should give them water, however—a dehydrated bird does not bleed out well.

Butchering Your Poultry

You have probably heard the phrase "running around like a chicken with its head cut off" as an apt description of someone who doesn't know what to do. Were you to cut the head off a chicken and then let go of the bird, it would flop around and scatter blood over quite a large area. This is certainly not the optimal way to butcher a chicken. However, no matter how you kill your chickens, there is going to be a certain amount of movement after the head is off and before the chicken is totally bled out, so be sure to wear old clothing and have a container ready to catch the blood. It's a good idea to have some water in the container so the blood doesn't coagulate in it and make cleanup harder. Keep in mind that even though the chicken's body may still be moving, the bird doesn't feel anything. What you're seeing is simply a nerve reaction.

The basic method for killing a bird is to either wring its neck or chop the head off. Then, make sure you hang it until it bleeds out, because bleeding out not only improves the flavor of the meat, but also increases its ability to be kept.

Self-Sufficient Facts, Knowledge, and Support

The average mature domestic turkey has approximately 3,500 feathers. Feathers cover most of a turkey's body, with the exception of the head and neck. These feathers can be cleaned and used to make a feather quilt or mattress.

Here are several different methods for killing a bird. Those described for chickens will work well for ducks, too, and those described for turkeys will work well with geese.

- Chopping block and a sharp ax—chicken or turkey: Lay the bird on a chopping block (you can pound two long nails about 1" apart halfway into the block as a stanchion for the head; just be careful you don't hit the nails with your ax). With one quick hit, bring the ax down and sever the head from the body. Then hang the chicken over a bucket to bleed out.
- Wringing the neck—chicken: Take hold of the chicken's head or upper neck and then swing the chicken around, as you would a heavy object on the end of a string. Swing several times until you hear or feel the "snap" of the chicken's neck breaking and separating from the body. You will then need to cut off the head and bleed the chicken.
- Hanging—chicken: Tie a piece of string or twine around a low-hanging tree branch. Take the other end of the string and loop it around the chicken's legs so it hangs head down. Take a sharp knife in one hand and grasp the chicken's head in your other hand. Pull slightly on the head and then cut the head off at the top of the neck. Have a container ready to catch the blood.

- A killing cone—chicken or turkey: A killing cone is one of the easiest ways to process your poultry. You can purchase a killing cone or make your own. You need a cone-shaped object, such as a 1-gallon bleach bottle or a road cone (depending on the size of the poultry you are processing) with both ends cut out. On one end, the opening should be about 2" in diameter—large enough for the bird's head and neck to slip through, but small enough so the rest of the bird doesn't follow. The other end needs to be large enough for you to be able to slip the bird inside, head first, but small enough so the bird's wings are pinned. The cone should be attached to a tree about 4 feet above the ground, or whatever is comfortable for your height. It can be attached with nails or screws, but it needs to be secure. You can create a cone stand with 3- to 4-foot lengths of two-by-fours fitted together like a pyramid with the cone held in the center for easy access. The cone should be attached so the smaller end, for the head, is closest to the ground. Place the bird in the cone, pull the head and neck through the cone, and then, using a very sharp knife, sever the jugular vein and carotid artery. The cut should be made just behind the tendon attachment for the beak and tongue. Cut deeply behind the jaw, pressing firmly with your knife while using a slicing motion. Cut down and toward the front of the neck, traveling under the jaw, and then cut the other side of the neck in the same location behind the jaw to sever the opposite blood vessel. Be aware that blood will spill onto your hands, and if you only knick the artery instead of cutting through it, blood will squirt out. Have a container ready to catch the blood.

For larger birds you can hook a metal weight to the lower beak of the bird after you have slit the throat. This holds the head, so the blood does not spray around the butchering area. Once the blood pressure drops, the bird will go into shock. As it dies, it will convulse and flap. Again, this is a nerve reaction to the loss of blood. At this point, the bird does not feel anything. The cone method helps to keep the bird relatively still during this process, so the meat is not bruised. You should spray the bird with water from a hose as it bleeds out to ensure the blood does not coagulate at the neck.

Picking the Poultry

You can choose, if you like, to just skin your poultry. This means you don't have to deal with scalding, plucking, or any of the traditional chores associated with dressing poultry. You can skin your poultry as you would a small animal.

If you choose to keep the skin on the meat, you will need a large container of hot water. A clean metal garbage can works well for this process. You will also need a gas burner to place under the can to keep the water at a constant temperature, between 135°F and 140°F (57°C and 60°C). If the water is colder than that, the scald doesn't work; if it is warmer than that, the skin can be damaged and the bird can be partially cooked.

Holding the bird by its feet, you should lower it headfirst into the scalding water. Do this slowly so you don't splash the hot water on yourself. Once the bird is in the water, you should move it up and down, swirling the water all around the bird. Make sure you keep the bird under the water to ensure even scalding, especially in the legs. Continue this process for about thirty seconds, and then pull the bird out and test the scald by rubbing your thumb against the grain of the feathers on the bird's leg. If you have scalded correctly, these feathers should come off easily. If your bird passes this test, pluck a large feather from the wing section. If this too comes out easily, you are ready to pluck the bird.

If the feathers don't come out easily, you need to scald the bird for a bit longer. However, remember that you don't want to expose the bird to too much heat, because it will damage the skin and make it easier to tear.

Self-Sufficient Facts, Knowledge, and Support
When processing turkeys, you should pluck the main tail feathers and the larger tail coverts before you dunk the bird in the scalding water. This makes it easier to see the bird as you work in the scald tank.

Move your bird to a processing table. Moving your thumb and fingers in a rubbing motion as you would if you were using sandpaper, remove the feathers by rubbing against the grain. This is more efficient than trying to pull out each individual feather. Don't yank a handful of feathers—this will only tear the skin.

The first feathers you pick should be the primary wing feathers. These will not be feathers that you are able to rub free. If you aren't able to grasp a feather and twist it until it breaks free, you might need to use a pair of pliers to get a good grip.

Clean all the feathers off the body, paying attention to the "wing pits" and any other crevices that might have hidden feathers, as well as any pinfeathers that lie just under the skin. When you have thoroughly cleaned the bird, spray it down with cold water from a hose and then submerse it in a clean container of very cold water in order to cool down the body quickly.

Dressing the Poultry

At this point, you are ready to clean the bird, which means that you remove the head, feet, and internal organs. Be sure you have a clean surface for this process, a very sharp knife, some clean water handy for rinsing, and a container for the discarded pieces.

Start by removing the feet. You need to hold the leg straight and, with just a little pressure, cut between the joints. You want to cut the tendons between the bones, not through the bone itself. The drumsticks will have some scaled skin on them; this won't affect the quality when you cook them.

Next, cut off the head. Cut the head with a sharp knife above the cuts you made to bleed out the bird. You should be able to cut right through a chicken's neck bone. However, with a turkey, you might need to use a cleaver.

After the head is removed, you should turn the bird onto its chest so you have access to the back. Insert your knife just under the skin at the base of the neck at the shoulders and slit the skin up the neck. Sliding the skin down, you will be able to see the trachea, esophagus, and glandular tissue next to the neck. Carefully separate the neck from the trachea and esophagus and gently loosen them all the way to where they enter the bird's body. If you follow the esophagus farther, it will widen into a pouch called a crop. Carefully separate the crop from under the skin and next to the breast meat. Then follow the trachea and pull off the fatty tissue from around the trachea and under the skin. Leave all these items hanging free for now.

Turn the bird over so it is lying on its back. Locate the vent between the legs. (The vent is the area where the bird emits eggs or droppings.) Insert just the tip of your knife into the skin about 1" above the vent. If you insert your knife too far you risk cutting the intestines.

Carefully cut up to the breastbone. Then carefully cut the area underneath the vent. You will want to take your time and not cut too deep. The vent has thin, tough tissue holding it in place, and you might need to work it loose with your fingers. If the bird was properly starved, there should be no feces inside the intestines; however, never take this for granted, and hold the bird slightly over the edge of the table to avoid fecal matter dropping on your work surface. Immediately clean up any spilled fecal matter.

With the vent cut free and loose from the body, you can gently pull the intestines free from the carcass. After they're removed, you can reach into the bird and move your hand along the sides of the ribs to break the entrails free of the body cavity. Once you locate the gizzard—a round, hard organ—pull it out. The rest of the entrails will come with it. Often, the esophagus and crop, as well as the trachea, will also follow the entrails when you pull the gizzard out.

Next, insert your hand back into the bird and follow the ribs to the spine. This is where you will find the lungs. They are quite spongy, so you need to carefully lift them out with your hands. Unfortunately, they don't always come out in one piece, so you need to continue until you don't feel any more lung tissue.

When the cavity is clean, turn the bird back on its chest and remove the neck. You should first cut the muscle tissue around the bone as far as you can. Then you need to bend the neck backward and break it off. It is better to break the neck than to cut it because the remaining edges will be less sharp, reducing the risk of puncturing the wrapping you will store your bird in when you freeze it.

Finally, on the other end of the bird are two small yellow oil glands, or preen glands. These glands should be carefully removed from the carcass. They are located inside the lump above the tail. Make an incision above the glands, cutting all the way to the bone, and then slide your knife along the bone, coming out at the tail. Be sure there is no yellow glandular tissue left, because it can foul the meat.

Rinse the bird thoroughly, inside and out. Put the bird into a tank of ice and water and let it chill for thirty minutes. Be sure the ice water also gets inside the body cavity so the entire bird is chilled.

Giblets

The giblets are the parts of the innards that you generally save and use for food. These usually include the heart, liver, gizzard, and neck. You've already harvested the neck, so just make sure it is rinsed thoroughly and placed in a plastic bag or container.

Self-Sufficient Facts, Knowledge, and Support
Chicken or turkey giblets are usually simmered in water for use in soups, gravies, or poultry stuffing. Once cooked, the liver will become crumbly, and the heart and gizzard will soften and become easy to chop. Cooked giblets should have a firm texture, and their juices should run clear. Casseroles containing giblets should be cooked to 160°F (71°C). Stuffing should be cooked to 165°F (74°C). Chicken giblets also are commonly fried or broiled.

The liver needs to be separated from the gallbladder. The gallbladder contains bile, an extremely bitter green fluid. You need to handle this carefully because if you break the gallbladder, the bile can contaminate the meat and cause it to be inedible. Cut the gallbladder away from liver, being generous with the amount of liver you leave on the cut, just to be sure. Then rinse the remaining liver and package it with the neck.

You should cut the gizzard open along its narrow edge. Slice down until you see a white lining. Try not to nick the yellow inner lining. Pull the gizzard apart with your fingers and remove the inner sac and white gizzard membrane and discard. If you cut into the lining, you will find grit and even rocks. The gizzard enables birds to chew their food. Simply remove the grit and peel the lining away from the muscle.

Cut the heart away from the attached arteries. Then you can slice the top off the heart, push out any coagulated blood, and rinse out any blood remaining in the heart chambers.

Rinse all giblets thoroughly, package them, and chill them in ice water for at least thirty minutes. Then dry them and package them with the bird.

LEARN TO BUTCHER LARGE DOMESTIC ANIMALS

When you are considering butchering large domestic animals, such as cows and hogs, you need to be sure you have the right equipment, the space to work, and an experienced friend to work with you. If you don't have someone with experience, you can either send your animals to a butcher who will kill them and then cut and wrap the meat for you, or you can buy a DVD that shows you the process in great detail. Because you have invested time and money into raising your domestic animals, you want to be sure that you are able to harvest the greatest amount of meat possible.

You should butcher when the weather is cool, on a fall day. Pick a location for butchering that has clean running water handy. Here are some items you will need if you are going to butcher your own meat:

- A .22-caliber (or higher) rifle or pistol (with cartridges) and good aim
- A block-and-tackle or strong rope and hoist to raise the animal, along with a large tree that has a strong limb from which to hang the carcass
- Some good sharp knives, a whetstone, and a meat saw
- A clean wood saw for cutting the animal in half

- Several 5-gallon buckets to hold the liver, heart, and any other organ meat you want to save
- A 50-gallon vat for scalding a pig
- A clean tarp or cloth to cover the animal after the carcass has been skinned
- A place to store the meat so it can age before it's cut
- A place to store the meat, such as a freezer or pantry, after it's been processed or canned
- Butcher paper, freezer bags, or freezer paper in which to store the meat
- A marker or labels to label the package with the date, cut of meat, and kind of meat
- A garbage can with liner for the butchering residue

You should butcher only healthy animals. If your animal seems unhealthy to you, have your veterinarian check it and treat it until it is healthy again. Don't eat an animal that has died unless the animal has died of an injury, such as getting hit by a car. Even in that case, if the animal has been dead for a while, don't eat it.

After your animal is butchered, check the meat carefully. Look for local bruises and injuries, abscesses, and single tumors. Those you can cut away from the meat and discard. However, if you find inflammation of the lungs, intestines, kidneys, inner surface of the chest or abdominal cavity, or numerous yellowish or pearl-like growths scattered throughout the organs (more likely in the case of sheep than cows or hogs), call your veterinarian and find out whether or not your meat is tainted.

When butchering hogs, you have a unique slaughtering decision to make. Because hog rind or skin is edible and generally considered a valued part of the meat you eat, hogs are scalded and then the hide is scraped. You scrape to get rid of not only the hair, but also dirt and scarfskin, or the top layer of skin. Keep in mind the size of the hog and the logistics of getting it into the scalding water, turning it over, and getting it out of the water. In order to scald the pig, you lower it into boiling water for about a minute, pull it up, and scrape it. You might need to lower it back into the water several times in order to complete the entire carcass.

Preserve Your Sustainable Lifestyle

After you process meat, you can use the hide to create skins and pelts for your own use. "Tanning" is a procedure that cures the hide and makes it soft, malleable, and beautiful. You can tan the skin of deer, rabbits, pigs, goats, and cattle.

The other option is to skin the hog. However, you will lose much of the valuable fat used to make bacon and lard. Whichever option you choose, remember that you can still use the pigskin not only as a food source but also for gloves and clothing. Once scraped or skinned, you will be able to process your pig.

BUILD A ROOT CELLAR

A root cellar is really nothing more than some sort of underground containment that maintains a certain temperature and humidity. If you have the time, space, and means to build a root cellar, you need to decide on its size and location.

Three examples of common root cellars are those built into the ground, into a hill, or into the basement of your home. There are advantages and disadvantages to each. If you build your root cellar into a hill, you can easily find the door even if there's 3 feet of snow on the ground. There also will be less chance of food damage from flooding or melting snow. Your cellar can be graded so any water that might run in or seep in will run out the door. However, a cellar in the side of a hill can be much more difficult to excavate.

A cellar built into the ground is easier to excavate, cheaper to build, and can be done in most landscapes. Also, a shelter can be built above it to make it more accessible in inclement weather.

Preserve Your Sustainable Lifestyle

Many older homes will have areas in the basements that already have earthen floors, designed for vegetable storage in the basement. You may already have a root cellar built in! Be sure to check before you start making plans.

You may find that the advantage of having a root cellar as part of your home is the convenience. You don't have to leave your house to obtain your produce.

However, before you construct a cellar, you have to be sure that you can maintain the humidity and the temperature needed in order to preserve your crops.

Ideal Root Cellar Conditions

You want the temperature of your root cellar to stay near freezing. Depending on where you live, that might not be a problem during winter months. But, a couple of sunny days might bring the temperature up as winter turns to spring. To avoid too much heat, borrow colder temperatures from the ground. Earth, even 2 feet down, has a remarkably stable temperature. The farther down you go, the more stable it is. You must go down a full 10 feet before complete temperature stability is reached, and for the average builder, depth is limited because of the expense of excavating. You can also borrow cool temperatures from the air. Often the nighttime air temperature will be cooler than the air in your cellar, so open a vent to take advantage of the cooler air. You should also think about the location of your root cellar in regard to passive solar heat. Build your root cellar in a place that is shady throughout the day and on the north side of your property, and use insulation to keep out the heat.

Your second most important consideration is humidity. Even if kept cool, vegetables will soften and shrivel up in a low-humidity environment. Most vegetables require high humidity. A typical underground root cellar will generally maintain a high humidity all by itself if it has an earth or dirt floor.

Preserve Your Sustainable Lifestyle

Keep shelves a couple inches away from the walls of the cellar to encourage air movement. Use wooden bushel baskets to hold your produce; they were actually invented for this purpose and they allow air to circulate from top to bottom.

Because the vegetables in your cellar give off gases that often are conducive to either spoilage or sprouting, you need to plan for good air circulation. Have an inlet vent and an outlet vent.

Avoiding Spoilage

Once produce is harvested it begins to decay. That's just part of the natural process. Certain microorganisms, including bacteria, viruses, yeasts, molds, and protozoans, cause the spoilage process. Microorganisms occur everywhere on the skin, in the air, in the soil, and on nearly all objects. It's important for you to remember that some of the conditions that accelerate spoilage, such as inappropriate temperature and moisture control, also encourage the growth of microorganisms that cause food-borne illness. Consequently, spoiled food is not just an issue of quality; it is also often a question of food safety.

The most common cause of spoilage in a root cellar is improper ventilation. Root cellars must have ventilation! This is one of the biggest mistakes people make when designing and installing them. Proper ventilation moves the ethylene gas that encourages spoilage away from the produce, increasing your storage time and the quality of the items in storage. It also slows down molds and mildews that thrive in dark, damp, still environments.

Although root cellars need to have some humidity, if temperatures start to rise, moisture coupled with heat will also cause plant deterioration and spoilage. Your root cellar needs to stay moist and at a temperature near freezing (32°F, 0°C) for most of your root vegetables. If you get much of a temperature fluctuation in your cellar, humid air will condense on the ceiling, walls, and the food you stored as the air cools to below its dew point. Excess water on produce can also encourage spoilage. Cover vegetables with burlap, towels, etc., to absorb condensation, and open the vents to get the air moving and remove the excess moisture.

COLLECT, SAVE, AND STORE SEEDS

When you look at a seed, especially an heirloom seed, you see more than the potential for a tomato plant or a head of lettuce. Rather, you can see generations of farmers cultivating, planting, and selecting the best of the yield—not to eat, but to save in order to harvest the seeds for the following year.

In most cases, you can save seeds from plants classified as annual (those whose life cycle lasts only one year) and biennial (plants whose life cycle lasts two years). The seeds you save from your garden have already become accustomed to your climate, your soil, and even the insects in your area.

Saving garden seeds at the end of each growing season can be a great cost-saving measure. It also assures you that the delicious tomatoes you loved from your garden, or the beans that produced so well, will still be around next year.

Hybrid Versus Heirloom Seeds

When you purchase heirloom seed, you are getting seed produced from plants that have been saved and grown fifty years or more, their seed passed down from generation to generation.

Hybrid seeds are created by plant breeders. These plant breeders select two similar plant varieties and crossbreed them to create a new plant variety that features traits from the two parent plants. For example, a plant breeder might select one plant that is frost resistant and another that has a sweeter taste. The new plant—the offspring of the two varieties—is now a unique hybrid variety that is both frost resistant and has a sweeter flavor.

Hybrid seeds are not bad in any way. They have helped increase crop yield and made it easier for many gardeners to be successful. However, hybrid seeds are not open pollinated. If you save their seeds, the forthcoming plant will not be identical to the parent plant. It might not be sweeter or frost resistant. Many hybrid seeds can be sterile and will not germinate. In order to have the same success you had with the initial offspring, you have to buy your seeds from the plant breeder again.

The beauty of an heirloom seed is the ability of the plant to change on its own. When you save heirloom seeds you select the one that ripened the fastest, was frost resistant, or was sweetest, and save its seeds. So, in time, the seed works through the same process as the hybrid, but it's a natural process. The offspring of that open-pollinated seed will produce the same results, or better, over and over again.

Collecting Seeds

As you work in your garden, you need to watch and see which of your plants you want to choose for seed saving. Once you choose the plant, you should do something to identify it so you don't accidentally harvest it. Whether you decide to place a certain-colored stake next to it or tie a piece of ribbon around its stem, be sure you share your plan with the other members of your family.

You want to pick the vegetable or fruit at the peak of maturity so your seed has the best chance of reproducing. There are three basic types of seed-bearing garden plants: fleshy fruits, seed crops, and those that scatter their seeds. When collecting the seeds of fleshy plants, such as tomatoes and peppers, you should allow the fruits to ripen, or even overripen slightly, before you collect the seed. But you don't want the fruit to blemish, mold, or shrivel around the seeds. You are still looking for a healthy parent plant.

When you collect from seed crops, such as corn, wheat, and beans, you want the plant to mature. These seeds will not deteriorate or blow away if the crop is left on the stalk or vine, as long as they remain dry.

Lettuce, onions, and broccoli are part of the group that scatters seeds. To be sure you capture the seeds from these plants, you can either watch them every day, collecting small amounts as they become available, or fashion a bag made of cheesecloth around the seed head to capture the seeds as they mature.

Self-Sufficient Facts, Knowledge, and Support
In nature, the vegetables and fruit you eat are, in reality, merely the food supply for the seeds inside. As the plant matures, the seeds inside become stronger and ready to survive on their own.

Extracting and Drying Seeds

When you extract the seeds from seed-containing fleshy fruits, you need to separate the seed from the pulp. If you've ever carved a pumpkin and cleaned it out, you will understand the process exactly. Once you've separated the seeds, wash them thoroughly and spread them out to dry. Large seeds can take up to a week to dry, smaller seeds half that long.

The best way for you to separate tomato seeds is to ferment them. The easiest way to do this is to slice open the tomato and squeeze the contents into a glass jar. Then you can add water to about halfway up the jar, stir, and set aside for a few days. A moldy residue will collect on the top of the water, as well as some tomato seeds. The tomato seeds that float to the top are worthless seeds. After about four days the water will clear and the good seeds will sink to the bottom of the jar. Discard the bad seeds and tomato pulp and place the good seeds on a paper towel to dry. Once dried, they can be removed from the paper and stored.

To extract the seed crop seeds, wait until the plants are fully dried and then twist them or pull their stalks through your hands to separate the kernels. Make sure they are dried and then store them.

The seeds you collected from the group that scatters seeds can be shaken through a hardware screen to ensure that pieces of chaff are not stored with them. Then dry and store the seeds. Be sure to give your seeds a long enough drying period. Storing seeds with a high moisture content will cause them to germinate poorly the following year.

Storing Seeds

You should store seeds in conditions that are cool, dark, and dry. Temperature fluctuations, especially heat, and humidity are seeds' worst enemies. Seeds do best at a moisture content of about 8 percent.

One way for you to ensure moisture content is to use a desiccant (a product used to remove excessive humidity) with your seed packets and seal them together in an airtight jar. A standard canning jar and lid, along with some silica gel, will do the trick. Add the silica gel to the jar; add the seeds, still in their packets, to the jars, and seal. Small seeds will dry down to 8–10 percent moisture overnight; large seeds may take several days. Seal the dried seeds in a new, dry jar and label it clearly. Then place it in a dark, cool place. You can even store seeds in your refrigerator or freezer.

CHAPTER 11
Tools for Farming and Repairs

Operating a self-sufficient home relies on your ability to maintain that home. As any homeowner can attest, owning your own home—no matter what the size—requires significant time and effort for routine maintenance as well as repairs, whether minor or major. You also need to be prepared to do extra work or hone specific skill sets, depending on the time of year or location of your home. (Indeed, the winter months can be particularly harsh on a northern home; late summer and fall hurricanes can take a toll on coastal homes; severe droughts can place a strain on your water supplies; and so on.) Owning and maintaining the right tools for your home and for all of your self-sufficient needs, whether for farming, structural repairs, or day-to-day upkeep, will keep you working efficiently, independently, and without the need to hire an outside contractor.

SET UP YOUR WORKSHOP

The proper hand tools will make your life so much easier, especially as you hone your homesteading skills. In fact, you'll find that owning a reliable set of tools will be an indispensable part of maintaining a self-sufficient home. From simple, quick fixes to longer-term upgrades and repairs, your tools will become old friends as your self-sufficient home continues to grow.

You may think that using a common hammer still requires plenty of effort. The fact is, the simplest tools are frequently some of the most labor-saving inventions, so it behooves you to have a good selection of hand tools, as well as a place to store, use, and repair them: that is, a workshop. You need a place indoors where you can perform tasks such as sharpening tools, replacing handles, and so on. The workshop doesn't need to be a large area, but in addition to the tool-storage area, you'll need a workbench large enough to accommodate whatever jobs will be brought indoors.

Self-Sufficient Facts, Knowledge, and Support
Just because your roof isn't leaking doesn't mean it shouldn't be maintained. Routine checks can mean the difference between minor repairs and major replacements. When maintaining your roof, keep these warning signs in mind: stains on your ceilings and walls; loose, cracked, and fallen shingles; mold and rot; ice dams, excessive condensation, or water in your attic after storms. If you notice these flaws, you aren't fully protected and should look into repairs or replacement.

Ideally, your home workshop should also have electricity, because you'll want an electric bench grinder to sharpen blades as well as a wire brush to clean the rust off of those same tools. If your self-sufficient home is totally off the grid, you could use a hand file and wire brush in place of electric tools. However, while you're doing these things, you'll want plenty of light for the job, as well as for finding things in the dark corners. Remember, although electricity isn't the only source of light indoors, it's probably the safest and most convenient. You'll need a bench vise to hold things securely in place while you're working on them, and you'll probably find that some sort of small anvil will be handy as well.

BUILD A TOOL COLLECTION ON A BUDGET

Like so many things, quality tools are expensive. However, there are still ways to furnish your workshop with a good selection of tools without spending a great deal of money, thanks in part to the fact that hand tools are so ubiquitous. In fact, they're so commonplace that many people who own them don't see a lot of value in the ones they have. That's why it's not unusual to see the metal heads of many tools simply thrown away if the handle breaks.

A double-bit ax blade doesn't seem like a particularly valuable commodity (especially when you don't need an ax), but a whole new ax will run you from $30 to $50, whereas, if you have just the ax head and a $6 hickory handle, plus the time to put the two together, you can make one that will work just as well as a new one.

You'll find that there are many perfectly good tool heads for shovels, rakes, picks, mattocks, hammers, axes—practically anything you care to name—lying someplace completely unused and unwanted. Abandoned buildings, flea markets, and your friends' garages are all likely places where you can find tool heads for free or for next to nothing.

Another excellent source of old hand tools, either whole or in parts, is the farm auction. Farmers leaving the country or retiring from farming generally divest themselves of their farming tools and equipment through auctions. You can often buy a lot containing several tools at once for a very low price at these auctions. Frequently the farmer will have a box or crate full of tool heads that you can buy, usually all in one lot, for next to nothing. In fact, after you've replaced a few handles, you may marvel that people would buy a new tool just because the handle breaks.

CHOOSE TOOLS FOR PLANTING AND FARMING

When choosing the tools or implements you will use for planting, gardening, and farming, a good rule of thumb is this: If it has a patent number, then Stone Age man probably didn't have one, and if he didn't, then you can probably get by without one as well. That's not to say that all advancements of the last ten millennia were without merit—steel shovels and plows are a nice upgrade from wood, which in turn was an improvement over the shoulder bones of an ox, but even steel tools aren't an absolute necessity.

If you're gradually transitioning to growing your own food, or just beginning to plant a garden, it's likely that you don't have all the tools that you may need, and you'll need to acquire a few. With that in mind, it is strongly recommended that you avoid new redesigns of old tools. If it doesn't look like what you've always considered a rake, a shovel, or an ax to look like, then it is probably inferior to the old standard. There are, of course, a few minor exceptions. For example, some of the ergonomically designed hand tools are easier

and more comfortable to use, and fiberglass handles are often superior to wood, even though you have to pay more for them.

Preserve Your Sustainable Lifestyle

Do your doors and windows feel particularly drafty?
Try adding vinyl weather stripping to those leaky spots
around your house. Use staples or nails to secure the
stripping every 6–8" around your window or door. If
you find that air is flowing in underneath your doors,
door draft snakes, or long bags filled with sand, can
be a quick and cheap way to block drafts. Insulating
drapes can be a decorative way to block unwanted air
and conserve energy.

AVOID PLASTIC OR STEEL TOOLS WHEN FARMING

It is both a curse and a blessing to live in modern times when so
many tools and materials are available. To ensure that this is more
of a blessing than a curse, you need to take a clear look at which
new innovations are genuine improvements, and which are simply
opportunities for manufacturers to fatten their bottom line by selling
you something. One of the most dramatic ways these innovations
have appeared is in the choice of materials used for any given job.
For most of history, steel and plastic were completely unknown, but
today, they are the most common materials used. There are several
good reasons for this from a manufacturer's standpoint, but they
don't necessarily translate into good reasons for your own home
repairs.

Let's start with plastic, the most modern of materials. Plastic definitely has a function in the gardening and farming world, particularly

because of its resistance to rot. If you need something that won't decompose quickly, then plastic may be the material for your job. It's often a good choice for buckets, tarpaulins, vapor barriers, and other such uses, but you need to remember that its strength is also its weakness; that is, it degrades very, very slowly, and when it does it breaks into flakes that can litter the landscape for years, decades even, after having lost its functional value.

Steel is about as strong as anything you're likely to encounter on the farm, but it's expensive. It may not be expensive to use in manufactured products—a steel chair may well be less costly than a wooden one—but it's expensive to use in crude situations, such as building fences.

Stone takes this calculation to extremes. As a raw material for fabrication, it can be extremely expensive to cut, smooth, and drill, but as a crude building material, you can have about all you want of it for free.

When money is in short supply, which it often is, it's a good idea to think about how farmers in history managed to cope when they needed to build something. If you do, you'll realize that you don't have to spend a lot of money to accomplish farming goals following the traditional methods.

MULTIPLY YOUR STRENGTH

Over the ages, some mighty impressive things have been done by men using no power source at all—just the strength of their muscles and those of their animals. They built the pyramids, paved the Appian Way, and cleared the American frontier.

Mostly they did these things with the simplest tools, such as the fulcrum, the pulley, and the lever. Farmers have been using some of these work-savers for thousands of years to turn themselves into virtual supermen.

Because hand tools are cheap and plentiful, you need to take advantage of the awesome strength they can bestow upon you. When your machinery fails you and you really need to get it out of the way, there's nothing handier than a lever. When you need to pull with the strength of five men, a pulley will help you do that. There are a few basic hand tools that belong on every farm, without which life would be more of a struggle. You'll create your own list in time, but the following sections will describe a good basic selection.

Preserve Your Sustainable Lifestyle

Many shutters on modern homes serve decorative purposes only. Why not install working shutters on your self-sufficient home? These durable workhorses will protect your windows during storms, hurricanes, and blizzards. Your initial investment in permanent shutters may be a bit dear, but it will be worth it when you are prepared if a storm rolls around. For a cheaper option, aluminum shutters are available, and can be installed quickly if you have precious hours before a storm hits.

BUY USEFUL HAND TOOLS FOR SELF-SUFFICIENT FARMING

The following list may be only an approximation of the one you would write after you've been farming for a while, because every farm and every farmer is different, but here you'll learn some of the most useful ways to multiply your strength and expand your capabilities. You'll develop a list of your own, of course, but chances are your list will include several of these items. Not surprisingly, most of these tools are so basic that they have been part of human existence since the dawn of time, and even in this day and age, when seemingly every task has been mechanized, they still remain as useful and essential as they were thousands of years ago.

The Pulley

The basic idea behind winches and pulleys is that of the block and tackle. Using them, you are trading weight lifted (or pulled) for the distance you have to pull it. For example, if you have a 100-pound weight on a rope with a single pulley between you and the weight, and you want to lift it 100 feet, then you'll need to put 100 pounds of force into pulling the weight up 100 feet.

This in itself will be an improvement, because pulling down on a rope is easier than pulling up. But if you add a second pulley, the weight is distributed between the two pulleys so that the effort to lift the weight is half what it was—now 50 pounds—but in order to lift it 100 feet, you'll need to pull 200 feet of rope. And so it goes: The more pulleys you add to the equation, the less effort is required to lift the weight, but the farther you have to pull the rope. Early cranes were built to do extremely heavy lifting using the principle of the block and tackle to achieve mechanical advantage thousands of years before the discoveries of electricity and internal combustion.

You can use these principles to your own advantage whenever you need far more strength than your muscles alone can provide. You could never, for example, pull a fence wire as tightly as it needs to be pulled just with the strength of your body; with a hand winch, or comealong, it becomes a quick and easy job.

If you have routine heavy-lifting jobs, particularly if you do all the heavy lifting in one place, such as loading heavy items into a second-story loft, you should have a block and tackle set or a chain hoist at the ready, but any backyard farmer needs a plain old comealong (also called a cable puller) in his toolshed. You'll find a broad selection of such portable winches on the market with various weight ratings, and of course various price tags. The weight ratings refer to the amount of weight that the cable can support, but the weak spot is in the handle of the device. If possible, opt for tubular handles over those made of laminated steel, as the laminated handles tend to bend laterally well before the stated capacity is reached.

The Lever
Sometimes trying to get a heavy implement attached to the back of your tractor can be a big job, especially if you have an older model

built before quick-hitch hardware was invented. You can't back the tractor up to it precisely enough, and every time you try, you wind up a few inches off. Unfortunately, even something as small as a 5-foot bush hog can weigh several hundred pounds. Luckily, the simplest tool imaginable can save the day in this case, and you can even make one for yourself. Start with a large steel rod 1½" or 2" in diameter by 5 or 6 feet long. Get a blacksmith to sharpen one end to a dull point and sharpen the other end to a dull blade.

Sometimes referred to as a "spud bar," this pry bar, when used as a lever, allows you to easily scoot the implement, 1" or so at a time, to exactly where you need it to be, and you won't even break a sweat. This is a good way to move just about anything heavy, from adjusting railroad ties in your raised bed to moving a vehicle that won't start. Depending on the thickness of the rod you choose, this device can weigh 20 or 30 pounds, so it can be useful in piercing heavy materials, or as a sort of battering ram when you want to move something out of the way.

Lopping Shears

When your property-management tasks move beyond simply mowing grass, your tool set needs to expand to include a strong pair of lopping shears, especially if maintaining an orchard is part of your duties. Like so many things, cheap loppers aren't cheap at all because they fail easily, and you can't buy replacement handles. Get a pair of high-quality loppers, and they'll last you a lifetime.

Most strong sets will claim to be able to cut limbs of 1½" to 2", but for a price you can buy models that are advertised as twice that powerful. This, of course, isn't a very scientific classification, as cutting a 2" pine limb is a much easier matter than bringing down a 2" oak bow, but you can count on the fact that long, strong handles and compound linkage will add to the loppers' capability. They're also handy for other cutting jobs, such as shortening a garden hose and clipping off overhead branches.

The High-Lift Jack

A high-lift jack is a standard item among off-road 4WD enthusiasts, who use them in a variety of ways to lift, pull, or move aside stuck vehicles in remote locations. This is about the only jack you'll find that can pick up the axles of a tractor without having to build a tower of blocks to support it. If you turn the upper jaw to the horizontal, you can squeeze two things together tightly or use the jack as a substitute for fence stretchers. If your truck gets stuck in mulch up to the axles, you can pick it up high and (very, very carefully) push the jack over so that the wheels land on solid, higher ground. You'll find the high-lift to be among the handiest tools you can have on the farm, because it allows you to pick up more than 4,500 pounds from 4½" off the ground up to nearly 4 feet in the air. Its basic advantage is that of the simple lever.

Always make certain that a high-lift jack is fully perpendicular when operating, and be especially mindful that you push the handle fully all the way down on each down stroke. If you don't, the handle can kick back with a tremendous force in the close vicinity of your face. The high-lift jack requires a certain amount of caution because it isn't all that stable, especially when picking something very heavy up very high. If you watch your fingers, toes, and the rest of your body and keep them clear of the device, you'll do things with this jack that you can't do with any other.

Bolt Cutters

Bolt cutters are a wonderful invention that allows you to do small miracles. Take, for example, another wonderful invention of the last half century: steel stock panels, those extremely heavy-duty portable wire fences designed to hold cattle, hogs, and other large, destructive critters without significant damage. These are very nice for their intended use, but are also quite handy for gates, trailer racks, and trellises, provided that you have some way of cutting them. To do this, you could use a hacksaw, or even a file, if you don't care much about how productively you spend your time. But if you have other things to do with your life, a hefty set of bolt cutters, say about 24" long, will snap through those steel rods as if they were butter. Bolt cutters are the tool of choice for cutting locks, chains, fences, cables, and, of course, bolts.

Self-Sufficient Facts, Knowledge, and Support

Cracks in your foundation—whether hairline or large stress cracks—must be properly patched and maintained if you wish to keep water, pests, and radon out of your home. Before patching, make sure the crack is completely dry, clean the area, and remove any debris. Be careful when applying the sealer, and make sure you are using the right sealer for your foundation type. If you are worried that your foundation cracks are too serious for you to tackle yourself, call a contractor to help you remedy major structural damages.

Pole Saw

If your property contains any trees, you desperately need a pole saw, even though you may not know it yet. In case you've never seen a pole saw, it is exactly what it claims to be: a curved saw blade on the end of a telescoping pole. Now, it may be that you've been living on your property some time and never thought that such a saw was a necessity, or you may never have thought about one much at all. However, when you begin to farm your land, you'll realize that many of your tree limbs are low enough to interfere with mowing or bush-hogging (they might be situated so that they threaten to sweep you off the tractor and into the path of the mower if you don't keep your wits about you).

A pole saw cures these problems semipermanently. If you have a large number of such overhanging limbs to eliminate, then you might consider renting a gas-powered version, but if you only have a few, or if you just want to keep up with the ones that grow out and develop over time, the simple pole saw is worth every cent of its low price. Not only is a pole saw cheaper than a new pair of glasses, it's cheaper than the ladder you'd need to buy in order to prune those limbs with a handsaw—and a lot cheaper than the hospital bill you'd get if you fell off the ladder pruning tree limbs with a handsaw.

Crowbar

The crowbar, or wrecking bar, is a major convenience for farmers (as well as cat burglars, who are more commonly associated with its use). The primary purpose of a crowbar is to pry things apart, and it certainly serves that end. The remarkable crowbar is a single tool that can be used in different ways that epitomize each of the three classes of levers.

It may be one of the simplest of the simple tools, but the crowbar's uses are beyond number. For example, a crowbar can be handy as a tool to make holes or furrows in the garden. It works great as the primary tool you'd use to dismantle old buildings and salvage the wood they contain without breaking any more timbers than necessary. It's invaluable for opening stuck windows or doors. A crowbar can also be a godsend when convincing lynch pins in a tractor

3-point hitch to do your bidding, or when you just need to create a little space between two very heavy items.

Large Pipe Wrench

There are a lot of instances around the farm when you need to grasp and turn a round pipe, shaft, rod, or dowel, and in nearly every case, a pipe wrench is the best tool to use to do it. If the cylindrical object you need to rotate is small enough, you can just use a pair of pliers, but when you need to turn large pipes or shafts, such as a PTO drive or a long-rusted irrigation pipe, then a large pipe wrench is what you have to have.

"Large" is of course a relative term. Pipe wrenches come up to 5 feet long, with gaping jaws that open to bite down on pipes of up to 8" in diameter. Needless to say, you'll pay a small fortune for one of these giant wrenches new, and there aren't many to be found used. However, a wrench of "only" 18" to 24" will still give you superhuman strength when it comes to turning things, and if that isn't enough, you can always employ the next item.

Cheater Bar

Let's say that you have your 60" pipe wrench gripping the 8" rusted well casing you want to turn, and even with a neighbor's help, the two of you can't seem to budge the thing a single millimeter. Are you going to give up? No, you simply "cheat."

The cheater bar is simply a long steel pipe fitted over the handle of the wrench to extend the effective handle length as much as you need to achieve the leverage that's required to break loose the pipe in question. This technique can be used on just about any sort of wrench whose handle will fit inside the pipe you pick. You can boom a tractor to a trailer so securely that the tires will flatten out. You can turn the largest, most rusted nut or bolt on the farm with ease.

In fact, a cheater will give you the strength of ten men, if that's what you need, and with it, the item that you want to turn will either behave the way you want it to, or break off completely.

 Self-Sufficient Facts, Knowledge, and Support
The use of a cheater bar can multiply your bare-handed strength so greatly that you may very well exceed the structural limits of whatever device you're working on. You may crack lug nuts, sever handles, or snap load binders by applying too much force. Be prepared to react (get out of the way) in case this occurs.

The Adze or Mattock

You may not be familiar with either the word "adze" or the word "mattock," but you've probably seen quite a few adze-mattocks in your life. As mentioned earlier in this chapter, the earliest digging tool was probably a sharp stick or bone. The first time a human tried to improve on the sticks and bones found lying on the ground, the result was probably the first adze, the basic design of which mimics the shape of the human hand digging into soft soil.

The adze is a horizontal blade (as opposed to the ax, a vertical blade) on a handle. When the adze is paired with an ax on a single tool head, that tool is referred to as a "cutting mattock"; when the adze is paired with a pick, that's known as a "pick mattock."

Perhaps because of its very basic nature, the adze is argu-ably the most useful hand tool on the farm, especially as a short-handled, one-hand tool. With it, you can chop into rocky soil and thick sod with ease, perhaps easier than with your spading fork, but you can also use it in fine garden soil where the broad blade can take the place of a simple garden trowel or, if sharpened, do a bang-up job of chopping weeds to shreds. Once you've had one around for a while, you'll wonder how you got by before.

Self-Sufficient Facts, Knowledge, and Support
The adze is a truly ancient tool and archaeologists have discovered examples dating back to the Mesolithic period. Once adzes were used in carpentry, shipbuilding, and making railroad ties; today they are used primarily in gardening and digging in hard ground and are referred to as mattocks.

DESIGN YOUR OWN OFF-GRID HOME

The first thing you need to decide when it comes to building your shelter is whether you are going to do it yourself or hire a contractor. If you have the skill set to do the job, including experience in the construction trades, building your own home can be a fulfilling experience. If you do not have the experience, you can make costly mistakes. However, there are many sources available to help you work through the process of building your own off-grid home.

If you are building to live completely off the grid, you will want a home that is energy efficient and as green as possible. Earthship Biotecture (*www.earthship.com*) provides an entire website explaining how to use recycled materials to create a self-sustaining green home. The architects at Earthship have developed technologies from solar lighting to geothermal heating to wastewater management that can be built into your off-grid home. Used tires provide a base for foundations and walls.

Greenhomebuilding.com (*www.greenhomebuilding.com*) offers potential off-grid homeowners "a wide range of information about sustainable architecture and natural building." Through this website, you can learn about alternative, natural, and recycled building materials including sod, compressed earth, plaster, straw, tires, recycled paper, cans, bottles, cordwood, and even corn cobs. You can also find building plans and reviews of books about green and recycled building options.

If done correctly, your off-grid home will not look like a traditional home found in most neighborhoods. Off-grid homes are often built into the land to take advantage of passive geothermal heating and cooling. They often have windows on the south side of the house, to add in passive solar capture, but don't have windows on the north side because of heat loss. Very often, off-grid homes are more compact, so you are not heating extra space. However, off-grid homes can also be works of architectural beauty, expressing your unique tastes.

CHAPTER 12
Preparing for Disaster

As someone who has established a self-sufficient lifestyle, you understand the world you live in has no certainties. Storms may damage your food and water supplies; a particularly harsh winter may readily deplete your heating sources; and a power grid failure can put a strain on even the most eco-friendly homes. The only thing you can do to protect your family is to be prepared for whatever eventually may happen. Indeed, this may be the reason you began a self-sufficient home in the first place. No matter your goals, it is imperative to be prepared for any situation. This chapter will suggest scenarios that will cause your family to rely on themselves and the emergency preparations you have made.

CREATE A SEVENTY-TWO-HOUR KIT FOR YOUR HOME

Prior to Hurricane Katrina, FEMA used to encourage people to have a seventy-two-hour kit for each member of the family, because it was assumed that within seventy-two hours, government agencies would be able to get to the scene of any disaster or emergency and bring aid. Katrina proved that when there is a disaster of large scale, or one that affects a large portion of the country, you might have to rely on yourself for more than seventy-two hours.

Preserve Your Sustainable Lifestyle

The U.S. Department of Homeland Security's Ready Campaign is designed to empower and educate citizens to prepare for the potential of an emergency, whether a terrorist attack or natural disaster, by following some basic steps. The Ready Campaign requires three simple actions: supply yourself with an emergency kit; have a plan for your family; and understand the kinds of situations that you'll need to prepare for, and how to react to them.

However, the idea of having a seventy-two-hour kit or a "bug-out bag" is still good. If you need to leave your home quickly, whether in case of fire, flooding, or other natural disasters, each family member can quickly grab his or her seventy-two-hour kit and have some supplies that will make being displaced a lot more tolerable. Each kit should be contained in something that is easy to grab and carry. It's best to have a container that's waterproof. Some people use five-gallon buckets for their seventy-two-hour kits, and backpacks are also often used. The following section provides some ideas of things you could place in your kit. Be sure to customize the list in order to meet the needs your family.

Food and Water

You should have a three-day supply of food and water, per person, that requires no refrigeration or cooking. If you prefer, a small water filtration device can take the place of three days supply of bottled water, which can be heavy to carry. Some ideas for food include:

- Beef jerky
- Hard candy
- Juice boxes
- Protein bars/granola bars
- Trail mix/dried fruit

Remember to create the bags to meet the needs of your family. If you have infants and use formula, be sure to include formula and diapers in one of the seventy-two-hour kits.

Preserve Your Sustainable Lifestyle

Not every emergency happens when everyone is at home. Have a contact number that all family members should call in case of emergency. Be sure every member of your family knows the phone number and has a cell phone, coins, or a prepaid phone card to call the emergency contact. If you have a cell phone, make sure you program your emergency contact as "ICE" (In Case of Emergency) in your phone. If you are in an accident, emergency personnel will often check your ICE listings in order to get in touch with someone you know. Make sure your family, especially your children, have ICE numbers in their phones.

Bedding and Clothing

Having warm, dry clothing and blankets is important during any emergency and can sometimes be the difference between life and death.

- Blankets and emergency heat blankets (the kind that keep in warmth)
- Change of clothing: inexpensive sweatshirts and sweatpants are excellent choices—and don't forget socks
- Cloth sheet: to place over you
- Plastic sheet: to lie on if the ground is damp or to shield you from rain
- Raincoat/Poncho: small emergency ponchos work well
- Undergarments

Be sure to keep your stockpile of clothing up to date as your family grows. The last thing you need when faced with an emergency is a set of clothing that doesn't fit your children (or you!).

Fuel and Light

Heating food/water and escaping from a dangerous situation at night are only two reasons to have sufficient fuel and light. Another is to provide comfort in a scary situation.

- Candles
- Flares
- Flashlights and extra batteries
- Lighter
- Waterproof matches

As with your other supplies, make sure your lighting materials are well maintained. Batteries can die, matches can get wet, and lighter fluid can evaporate. Well-stocked and well-cared-for supplies will make an enormous difference in life-or-death situations.

Miscellaneous Equipment

These are some of the items that will make life much easier in case of emergency.

- Ax
- Can/bottle opener
- Dishes/utensils
- Duct tape
- Pen and paper
- Pocketknife
- Radio (with batteries)
- Rope
- Shovel

Be wary of where you store these materials if you have little ones. While they are emergency essentials, they should be kept away from youngsters and curious hands. Make sure they are accessible for adults, but tucked safely away from children.

Personal Supplies and Medication

You can't take your bathroom medicine cabinet with you, but you should be sure you have the life-sustaining medical supplies you need during an emergency.

- Cleaning supplies (mini hand sanitizer, soap, shampoo, dish soap, etc.)

- Extra pair of glasses
- First-aid kit and supplies
- Medicine (acetaminophen, ibuprofen, children's medication, etc.)
- Prescription medication (for three weeks or more)
- Toiletries (roll of toilet paper—remove the center tube to easily flatten into a zip-top bag—feminine hygiene, folding brush, etc.)

Having medical, cleaning, and personal hygiene supplies will bring comfort to your family during stressful times. Make sure all medications are up to date, and that they haven't passed any expiration dates.

Personal Documents and Money

If your home was devastated by a flood or fire, what legal documents would you need as you put your life back together? Here's a list of some of the items. You might think of others that are important to you. Place these items in plastic bags so they are waterproof.

- Cash
- Copies of insurance policies
- Copies of legal documents (birth/marriage certificates, wills, passports, contracts, etc.)
- Copies of vaccination papers
- Credit card

Remember to update your kits to make sure all food, water, and medications are fresh and not expired, that the clothing still fits, that the personal documents and credit cards are up to date, and that the batteries are charged.

Self-Sufficient Facts, Knowledge, and Support
The Ready Campaign, FEMA, Citizen Corps, American Red Cross, and the Humane Society of the United States have developed an emergency preparedness toolkit for your pets. This toolkit can be found at *www.ready.gov/america/toolkit_pets/index.html*.

MAKE SURE YOU HAVE CLEAN WATER

Having an ample supply of clean water is a top priority in an emergency. A normally active person needs to drink at least two quarts of water each day. If an emergency occurs in the summer, or if you live in a hot or arid environment, you will require more. In all cases, children, nursing mothers, and ill people will require more than two quarts of water a day. Because you will also need water for food preparation and personal hygiene, you should store one gallon per person per day. FEMA recommends that, if possible, you store a two-week supply of water for each member of your family. And if supplies run low, don't ration water. Drink the amount you need today, and try to find more for tomorrow. You can minimize the amount of water your body needs by reducing activity and staying cool.

Store drinking water in food-grade containers. Two-liter plastic soft-drink bottles work well. You can store water to be used for personal hygiene, flushing toilets, and general cleaning in old bleach and laundry detergent containers.

To prepare your own stored water supply, see the following tips, as suggested by FEMA.

1. Thoroughly clean the bottles with dishwashing soap and water, and rinse completely so there is no residual soap.

2. Additionally, for plastic soft-drink bottles, sanitize the bottles by adding a solution of 1 teaspoon nonscented liquid household chlorine bleach to a quart (¼ gallon) of water. Swish the sanitizing solution in the bottle so that it touches all surfaces. After sanitizing the bottle, thoroughly rinse out the sanitizing solution with clean water.

3. Fill the bottle to the top with regular tap water. If your water utility company treats your tap water with chlorine, you do not need to add anything else to the water to keep it clean. If the water you are using comes from a well or water source that is not treated with chlorine, add two drops of nonscented liquid household chlorine bleach to each gallon of water.

4. Tightly close the container using the original cap. Be careful not to contaminate the cap; do not touch the inside of it with your fingers. Write the date on the outside of the container so that you know when you filled it. Store in a cool, dark place.

5. Replace the water every six months if not using commercially bottled water.

During an emergency, remember that you can use some of the "hidden" sources of water in your home, including your hot-water heater, accumulated water in your pipes (accessed by unscrewing a pipe in the lowest area of your home, such as a basement), and water from ice cubes in your freezer. You should not drink the water from toilet flush tanks or bowls, radiators, waterbeds, or swimming pools and spas.

If you use the water in your hot-water tank, be sure the electricity or gas is shut off, and then drain the water from the bottom of the tank. When the power and/or water is restored, be sure to fill your tank back up before turning on the power.

You can also find water outside your home in case of emergency. Rainwater, streams, rivers and ponds, natural springs, and lakes are other sources for water. Never take water from places that have material floating on top, or that have an odor or dark color to them. Never drink flood water. Water that you have gathered from the outdoors needs to be treated before you can safely drink it. There are several ways to treat water:

■ If you decide to chlorinate the water you have gathered from your water source, you should add sixteen drops (⅛ teaspoon) of bleach per gallon of water. Stir the water thoroughly and then let it stand for thirty minutes. Once the time has passed, smell the water. You should be able to smell the bleach. If you can't, add an additional ⅛ teaspoon bleach per gallon, mix thoroughly, and let it stand for another fifteen minutes. Once again, smell the water. If it still does not have a slight odor of bleach, discard it and find another source of water.

■ The safest way to treat water is to boil it. However, you must remember that boiling does not mean a bubble or two. When you boil water, you must bring it to a rolling boil for at least one full minute. If you are concerned about evaporation, you can place a lid on the pot to capture the steam. After boiling, place the water in a clean container and allow it to cool. For better-tasting water, you can return oxygen to it. To do this, simply pour the water back and forth between two clean containers. The movement of the water between the containers will increase the oxygen content. This method also works for stored water.

- Use a ceramic filtration system to filter out unhealthy microorganisms.

To remain truly self-sufficient, keep an ample supply of clean, safe drinking water for you and your family. You'll have peace of mind knowing you are fully supplied, in case disaster strikes.

HAVE A BACKUP HEAT SOURCE

It's the middle of winter and a major ice storm has swept through not only your state, but also an entire five-state region. Electric lines are down and hundreds of thousands of people are without power. You live in a rural community, so you are among one of the last groups that get power restored. The temperatures outside are in the single digits and the wind chill is making it even colder. What are you going to do?

If you are totally self-sufficient, life goes on as usual. But, if your self-sufficient lifestyle still relies on local utilities, some of these ideas might save your life.

Wood Stoves

If you have already installed a wood stove, you have both an alternative heat source and a way to cook for your family. Wood stoves need no electricity to run and can warm just one room or, in some cases, an entire house. With a wood stove you can also use nonelectric heat-powered fans that can sit on the stove and move the heat throughout the room. As mentioned earlier in this book, wood stoves are more efficient than fireplaces because they don't pull warm air out of the house.

Propane Heaters

Portable propane heaters are another good option for emergency home heating. The advantage of a propane heater is that propane is easily stored and, if you have a propane grill, you may already have a tank on hand. Propane is clean burning with little odor and is relatively safe. Because portable propane heaters are unvented, you must crack open a window. If you use a larger, 20-pound tank to run the stove, it is recommended that you place the tank on the outside of the house and run an extension hose from the tank to the stove. A portable propane heater puts out about 9,000 BTUs (British thermal units), which is enough to heat one medium-sized room. Larger propane heaters can put out about 12,000 BTUs.

Self-Sufficient Facts, Knowledge, and Support

When you choose a portable heater, purchase one approved by a nationally known safety-testing laboratory, such as Underwriters Laboratories or Factory Mutual Research Corporation. Look for a heater with a broad, solid base, as well as an automatic cutoff switch, which trips when a unit is tipped over. Thoroughly read all manufacturers' instructions about the installation and use of portable heaters. Keep the instructions in an accessible place so you can reread the operating and safety precautions every year.

Kerosene Heaters

Portable kerosene heaters are one of the most popular ways to provide emergency home heat. Most modern kerosene heaters are safe, but you still need to keep a window cracked open to prevent carbon monoxide buildup. Kerosene heaters are generally round, with a wick that pulls up the fuel and burns it to create heat. Newer models have an automatic shutoff system in case the heater is tipped over. Some models have a battery-powered ignition to light the wick.

Kerosene heaters produce a slight odor, mostly when they are extinguished. Floor-standing kerosene heaters can put out 20,000 BTUs or more, enough to keep a modest-sized home warm. If this is your choice of emergency heat, you will have to be sure you keep a supply of kerosene on hand.

Your Own Furnace with a Generator Backup

Even if you have a gas, liquid propane, or oil-fired furnace, you might still need electricity to start the pilot light or make the blower work. In order to use your furnace during a power outage, you will need a backup generator. Have an electrician add a bypass switch and connection for the portable generator. At the least, you will need a 5-kW generator, which will also be able to power some other circuits, including a fridge and lights; however, it will not likely be able to power your whole house. Expect to spend at least $3,000 on a generator, plus the bypass box and electrician's fees.

KEEP THE LIGHTS ON

Emergencies can happen in the middle of the night, and that is not the time to start searching for flashlights, batteries, or other light sources. To be prepared, you need to have immediate light sources and potential long-term light sources.

Flashlights

Flashlights are great for a quick response to an emergency situation. The more reliable flashlights are LED flashlights because incandescent bulbs can burn out suddenly or break if you drop your flashlight. LED flashlights don't have breakable parts and last for about 10,000 hours of use.

If you purchase an inexpensive flashlight, the light will not be as bright and might be slightly off-color. There are many different shapes and styles of flashlights, but the major differences are the size and weight of flashlight you want to carry, as well as the brightness you desire.

- Key-ring flashlights are generally more gimmicky than useful. They can fit in your pocket or your purse and weigh next to nothing, but most give barely enough light to see a few feet in front of you.
- Pocket flashlights are a good choice for emergency. The better-quality flashlights are able to regulate voltage, so even when the battery is losing power, the light will remain bright. They are small enough to carry in a pocket, purse, or backpack, or to put in a drawer in your nightstand.
- Glove compartment flashlights are too large to easily fit in your pocket and too heavy to carry in your purse or backpack. The best ones provide you with an adjustable high and low beam: the low beam for use inside the car, and the high beam for lighting the outside of the car in emergencies.
- Emergency crank flashlights are excellent tools for emergencies. Not limited to the charge of a battery, they are small enough to fit in a glove compartment and can run thirty to

sixty minutes after one minute of cranking. Often these flashlights include other options, such as weather radios.

■ Large household flashlights are heavy and can be cumbersome, but they provide a great deal of light when you are trying to find your way through your home in a power outage.

■ Rechargeable flashlights are great while you still have power or, if they are solar powered, while there is sun available, but they lose their power fairly quickly compared to other choices. A rechargeable flashlight is best used in areas where a sudden power outage can be dangerous or frightening, for small children in a bathroom, for instance, because they are easily located.

Experts recommend lithium-ion-powered flashlights for use in very cold weather and for flashlights stored in a disaster shelter because they last for a longer period of time under harsher circumstances.

Candles

Using candles for emergency lighting is one of the least expensive lighting options. Candles that come in glass containers are the best kind to have in case of emergencies. Regular dinner tapers or pillar candles don't put out the kind of light you need and can be dangerous if left unattended. Emergency candles are long burning. There are even some 120-hour versions, and they are constructed for safe burning.

When using any kind of candle, be sure it is situated on a stable surface that is free from clutter. Because a quick draft can cause a candle flame to jump, never put a candle near curtains or any other flammable objects.

You can also use candle lanterns to increase the safety of using candles. Lanterns provide a base, a lid, and a glass surround or chimney in which to place the candle. They also provide a carrying handle, so the candle can be safely transported without fear of the flame being blown out. Some lanterns designed for camping and outdoor use can hold a standard white emergency candle, which can burn for eight or nine hours.

A candlelier is a lantern that holds three standard emergency candles. The candles can be burned individually or simultaneously, depending on the amount of light you desire. The top of the lantern has a heat shield that can also be used as a small stove. Candleliers also produce enough heat to be a personal heat source.

Lanterns and Oil Lamps

Lanterns and oil lamps are another option for lighting your home during an emergency. Lanterns have been used throughout the world for centuries to provide portable light. Generally, kerosene or specially made lamp fuels are used for lanterns. You can purchase an inexpensive oil lamp that uses paraffin oil at most department stores. These are mostly ornamental, although they give enough light to see and can be placed throughout your home when not in use as part of the décor. Both of the aforementioned fixtures generally use wicks to pull the fuel up from the base and feed the flame. Specialty lamps such as Aladdin lamps use mantles and kerosene fuel. The light from an Aladdin lamp is equal to a 50-watt light bulb.

HAVE MEDICINE AND FIRST-AID SUPPLIES ON HAND

You should have an ample supply of over-the-counter medicines for emergencies. If you rely on prescription drugs for your health and well-being, you should also try to keep at least an additional three-month supply of them in your home. Talk to your physician about writing an additional prescription to ensure you can have an extra supply in case of emergency.

Here is a list of some of the basic over-the-counter medicines and medical equipment you should have in your home:

- Antacid (Tums, Rolaids)
- Antibiotic cream such as Neosporin or Betadine
- Antidiarrheal medicine
- Bandages, Ace bandages, adhesive tape
- Cotton balls and swabs
- Cough syrup, cold/allergy medicine, antihistamine, and decongestant
- Ear drops
- Eye cup and over-the-counter eye wash
- Heat pack and ice pack
- Hot-water bottle
- Hydrocortisone cream
- Hydrogen peroxide
- Itch medicine (calamine lotion)
- Mild laxative
- Pain relievers such as acetaminophen, aspirin, naproxen, and ibuprofen
- Petroleum jelly
- Rubbing alcohol
- Sunscreen
- Syrup of ipecac (to induce vomiting)
- Thermometer
- Tweezers

During times of stress or emergency, it can be difficult to treat wounds or illness if you're not sure what you have on hand. Keep your medical supplies together, kept away safely from young children, and up to date. That way, you'll always be prepared.

Medicinal Herbs as Backup

If you find yourself in an emergency situation without the medical supplies you need, your herb garden may be a valuable source to treat ailments and problems until you can get the supplies you desire. Here is a list of common ailments and a sampling of herbs that have medicinal properties for those problems:

- Anxiety: ginger, marjoram, rosemary, spearmint, and St. John's Wort
- Bladder problems: lavender and St. John's Wort
- Bug bites: safflower and sage
- Colds and sore throats: bee balm, cilantro, dill, ginger, marjoram, periwinkle, spearmint, and thyme
- Digestive problems: angelica, bee balm, cilantro, ginger, lavender, parsley, sage, and spearmint
- Fevers: cilantro, lavender, and safflower
- Flatulence: dill, fennel, and sage
- Migraines/headaches: angelica, marjoram, and rosemary
- Ulcers: angelica, periwinkle, aloe
- Wounds/muscle aches: comfrey, garlic, and thyme

As you gather supplies to create your seventy-two-hour kit, check with your doctor to make sure you or a family member do not have any allergies to any particular herbs. Keep a list of potential allergens in your medical kit to be safe.

KEEP YOUR PANTRY STOCKED

During emergencies you don't want to give your system a shock by eating foods you have never tried before. Your emergency supplies should include foods such as peanut butter that are easy to use and offer you high protein. Make sure you try out your emergency supplies if you are going to use foods such as Meals, Ready to Eat (MREs) and dehydrated foods before an emergency happens.

If your activity is reduced, you can survive on half your usual food intake for an extended period and even go without any food for many days. Food, unlike water, may be rationed safely, except for children and pregnant women. If your water supply is limited, don't eat salty foods, as they will make you thirsty. Instead, eat salt-free crackers, whole-grain cereals, and canned foods with high liquid content.

MREs and Dehydrated Foods

MREs were originally government-issued dehydrated meals developed for soldiers. Although the government does not allow military MRE manufacturers to sell to civilians, there are MREs available for sale to the general public. The positive aspect of an MRE is that it is a complete meal in one package that is designed to withstand the elements. Each package generally contains an entrée, side dish, cracker or bread, spread, dessert, candy, beverage, seasoning or hot sauce, plastic ware, and a flameless ration heater. Each MRE contains one-third of a day's nutritional value, with 1,250 calories and mineral and vitamin supplements. The downside of MREs is that they can be expensive and there are limited menus available in the retail versions.

Dehydrated foods have come a long way in the past twenty years. Originally very simple and bland, dehydrated food now comes in a great variety of offerings, including gourmet foods. You can purchase dehydrated foods in large number ten cans—the size of a coffee can—to feed your whole family, or in individualized single meals. As the name implies, all you have to do is reconstitute the food with water and then heat it. Dehydrated food can have a shelf life of eight to ten years.

Family Friendly Foods

If you have children, your emergency food stores should include food that is familiar and comforting. Peanut butter, macaroni and cheese, pudding, and powdered drink mix can lend an air of normalcy to a tense situation. Be sure to have crackers and hard candy in your emergency food supply for treats. Powdered chocolate drink mix can help turn nonfat dry milk into a more palatable drink for both children and adults.

Maintaining Your Strength

During and especially after a disaster, it is vital for you to maintain your strength. Be sure that you eat at least one well-balanced meal each day, drink enough liquid to enable your body to function properly, and take in enough calories to enable you to do any necessary work. Vitamin, mineral, and protein supplements are essential during times of high stress on your body; don't forget to take them.

PRACTICE EMERGENCY COOKING

During an emergency, providing hot meals for your family can be a challenge. But in order to avoid making a stressful situation even worse, proper nutrition and some kind of routine is good for your family. In order to conserve your cooking fuel, you need to be as efficient as possible. Only boil the amount of water you are going to need. Put out the fire as soon as you have finished cooking. Plan your meals ahead of time to consolidate as much cooking as possible. Use the top of your heating unit, if possible, to cook your meals.

Always keep enough fuel, including charcoal and liquid propane, to allow you to cook outdoors for at least seven to ten days. Use Dutch ovens and pressure cookers to optimize the use of fuel.

Store matches in a waterproof, airtight tin with each piece of equipment that must be lit with a flame. Other options for cooking during an emergency include the following.

Camp Stove

Camp stoves provide a perfect alternative when home electric or gas stoves are inoperable. A two-burner camp stove is a compact, portable, and convenient means to provide hot meals and hot drinks for days on end if necessary. Models are available that run on propane or liquid camping fuel (sometimes called white gas). In addition, some models can run on either liquid camping fuel or unleaded gasoline. Fuel-powered camp stoves must never be used indoors.

Sterno Fuel

Sterno fuel, a jellied petroleum product, is an excellent source of cooking fuel. Sterno is lightweight and odorless, and can be easily ignited with a match or a spark from flint and steel. It is not explosive and it's safe for use indoors. You can purchase Sterno stoves at any sporting goods store for a relatively small amount of money. The stoves fold up into small, compact units.

Sterno is ideal for carrying in a pack. The fuel is readily available at all sporting goods stores and many drugstores. One can of Sterno fuel, about the diameter of a can of tuna fish and twice as tall, will allow you to cook six meals if used frugally.

 Self-Sufficient Facts, Knowledge, and Support
Sterno fuel was invented around 1900. Made from ethanol, methanol, water, and a gelling agent, it also contains a dye that colors it pink. A 7-ounce container will burn for as long as two hours.

The disadvantage of Sterno is that it will evaporate easily, even when the lid is securely fastened. If you store Sterno, you should check it every six to eight months to ensure that it has not evaporated beyond the point of usage. Because of this problem, it is not a good fuel for long-term storage. It is very expensive to use compared to other fuels available, but is extremely convenient and portable.

Charcoal

Charcoal is the least expensive fuel per BTU to store. However, charcoal can only be used outdoors because of the vast amounts of poisonous carbon monoxide it produces. Charcoal will store for extended periods of time if it is stored in airtight containers. Because it can easily absorb the moisture from the air, it should not be stored in the paper bag it comes in for more than a few months. Transfer it to airtight metal or plastic containers and it will keep almost forever. If you store $50–$60 worth of charcoal, you will have enough cooking fuel for a family for an entire year if used sparingly.

You can use charcoal in a traditional grill, hibachi, or with a Dutch oven. A Dutch oven is a cast-iron pot with a lid that can come in various sizes and can be used over an open fire. When you combine a Dutch oven with charcoal, you are able to create stews, soups, and even baked goods. Each briquette will produce about 40° of heat. If you are baking bread, for example, and need 400° of heat for your oven, simply use ten briquettes.

STORE YOUR DOCUMENTS PROPERLY

From birth certificates to passports, from insurance policies to car titles, many of the documents you have in your home are very important, but could be lost during a fire, flood, or other disaster. It is a good policy to make several copies of these important documents. The original copies should be kept in a safe-deposit box in a bank; another copy could be given to family members who don't live in your household; another copy should be filed away in your home office; and the final copy should be laminated and stored in your seventy-two-hour kit. If an emergency arises and you have to leave your home, all of your important documents are with you.

Ultimately, your preparedness for disaster lies in your ability to plan ahead. Keeping copies of up-to-date records will ensure your financial safety and give you peace of mind. Planning ahead for all items in your seventy-two-hour kit, from medical supplies to heat and light to food and water, will give you an edge during an emergency, help keep you safe, and potentially buy you more time until rescue crews arrive or power is restored. And during an emergency, that's what being self-sufficient is all about.

INDEX